The Rock is a small town in the Riverina region of southern rural New South Wales, Australia. The town derives its name from The Rock Hill which was, for thousands of years, known as "Kengal" by the local Wiradjuri people and which held, and continues to hold for them, spiritual significance. The hill was first observed by Captain Charles Sturt on his epic river journey down the Murrumbidgee River in 1829. The nearby town that grew with white settlement originally became known as "Hanging Rock" because of a large rock which appeared to be "hanging" on the top of the hill. This rock displaced and fell in 1874 so it is somewhat baffling as to why the town was officially gazetted as Hanging Rock, some 8 years later in 1882, when there was no longer a hanging rock! Sensibly, at some point thereafter, the town simply became known as The Rock.

The Rock-Yerong Creek Magpies are the local footy team and they play home games at Victoria Park, which is the town recreation oval [yes, another black and white Aussie Rules team with a home ground called Victoria Park].

Yerong Creek is an even smaller town about 13 kilometres south of The Rock on the Olympic Highway towards Albury/Wodonga. The local footy side merged with The Rock's in 1962 and the merged team became known, for a time, as The Combines. The senior team was largely unsuccessful until 1986 when it won a long-awaited and very close Grand Final against its arch enemy, Mangoplah-Cookardinia United. Over the next 29 years, the team made up for the previous long period of non-success by winning 8 premierships.

A Band from The Rock

The story
of
The Mystics
and
Collection

1965 – 1969

A Band from The Rock

First published in Australia by Peter L Brown 2021

Copyright © Peter L Brown 2021
All Rights Reserved

A catalogue record for this
book is available from the
National Library of Australia

ISBN: 978-0-646-84779-5 (pbk)

Typesetting and design by Publicious Book Publishing
Published in collaboration with Publicious Book Publishing
www.publicious.com.au

No part of this book may be reproduced in any form, by photocopying or by any electronic or mechanical means, including information storage or retrieval systems, without permission in writing from both the copyright owner and the publisher of this book.

Dedicated to the friendship, musicianship and memory of
Patrick James Geaghan
9th November 1948 – 19th October 2020

Author's Note

At the onset of Covid-19 in March 2020 and the lockdowns that followed, I decided to isolate at our beach house in Bermagui on the south coast of New South Wales. Because of limited activity options associated with the lockdown, I needed something to do to fill in the long hours of each day. This story was originally to be a brief history of both bands which was to be handed out to the punters at a 2005 band reunion concert. Due to the many other matters I had to attend to in organizing the reunion, whilst started, the story never got any further and was therefore never handed out.

It remained in a file on my laptop for 15 years until one day in lockdown, I was tidying up the files and came across the unfinished story and thought that finishing off the story was exactly what I needed to kill lockdown time. As I gathered information for the story, it soon became apparent that our memories were less than reliable, so I decided to utilize wider research to fill in the gaps and the brief history suddenly took on a life of its own and became a full-blown storied history!

The end intention was to simply hand out copies to my old band mates, relatives, some close friends, past fans and to be used as a display and reference item in the local museum. What follows has been written specifically for these people consequently it assumes that the reader is acquainted with places, people and events mentioned in the story, which to any other reader, will mean nothing.

It was only after completing the story that I was encouraged to make it available to a wider readership and thankfully, I found a supportive publisher.

Contents:

Acknowledgements		i
Introduction		iii
Band Members Guide		vi
Chapter 1	Pre-1965	1
Chapter 2	1966	5
Chapter 3	1967	18
Chapter 4	1968	31
Chapter 5	1969	52
Chapter 6	Not the final Chapter	74
Chapter 7	The day after – and why I bothered!	81
Chapter 8	Postscripts	85
Chapter 9	Photos and Gig Ads	88
Chapter 10	Gig Towns, Venues and Dates	92
Chapter 11	More photos and Gig Ads	101
Chapter 12	Odds and Sods and other stuff	115

Acknowledgements

During my research I used the following resources and/or people who were extremely helpful in arranging for me to view old newspapers or microfilmed copies in their possession or to which they had access, and for this I thank them.

CSU Regional Archives, Wagga Wagga
Les Dale, Henty
Tumut Library, Tumut
Broadway Museum, Junee
Peter Mahony, Temora and the *Temora Tribune*
Colin Weise and Green's Gunyah Museum, Lockhart
National Library, Canberra

Unfortunately, I can't say the same about the Tumut office of the Tumut and Adelong Times, where I was led to believe copies of the Tumbarumba Times were located. The owner, despite initially saying [unconvincingly] that he would get back to me about accessing the papers, did not, and subsequent follow-up on a number of occasions was met with the same unsuccessful response necessitating a trip to the National Library in Canberra to access microfilm copies of the paper!

I also would like to acknowledge the information and memories provided by Keith Bird, Wagga's leading dance and band promoter during the years that this story covers and who booked both The Mystics and Collection for many gigs at Kyeamba Smith Hall, The After 5 Club and Griffith.

Terry Stirzaker, Mick Archer and Peter Quine all provided information in varying degrees and Sue [Manning] Hancock supplied photos and gig ads of Collection - for their interest, I extend my thanks and appreciation.

And finally, to my old band mates through both bands – it was a struggle to remember what happened back in those days but between us I've managed to glean enough from our largely forgotten band days to add extra colour to the story. I am sure there are things that should be in this story but our collective failure in the memory department will ensure that they will forever remain in the past. Anyway, there is enough in the following pages to allow the reader a reasonable insight into what it was like to be young and let loose into the local music scene that was so vibrant in the mid to late 1960's.

A Band from The Rock
[The only real "rock" band]

It's not a "warts and all" story because some of the warts
have been cut out - deliberately!

Introduction

Music means various things to people – from having no interest in it at all [a musical agnostic], having an interest that stops at only having an interest [an interested listener], or having an interest that leads to a committed involvement [a musician]. The main people in this story fall into the last category.

This is a storied history of a band from late 1965 to late 1968, which started from nothing in The Rock, a small regional town in New South Wales, during the mid-1960's pop music explosion, got better and better, changed its name towards the end of 1968, and was eventually voted the best band in Wagga Wagga, the largest regional city in New South Wales, towards the end of 1969.

The Mystics

This is the story of The Mystics in the years between late 1965, when the band formed at The Rock, and up until the band changed its name in late 1968. It is based on the recollections of members that made up the original group and also includes those of Des Condon, who was briefly in the band at the start, Pat Geaghan who replaced Les Magrath in late 1967, Garry McKenzie, who replaced Col Moore briefly in 1968, and to a very limited extent, Robert Kitney, who replaced Dennis McGrath for a brief period also in 1968.

Collection

The account of Collection relates to the period after the name change from The Mystics in the latter part of 1968 following which Colin Moses replaced Colin Moore and up until the end of 1969 when Dennis McGrath and I, the last remaining original members from The Rock, left thus ending the connection the band had with The Rock.

The information and events contained herein have been ascertained from individual band members, band group discussions [and sometimes spirited arguments], people who were fans of the band, research in Wagga, Lockhart, Tumut, Henty, Junee, and Temora local papers, either in hard copy or microfilm, research at the National Library Canberra for Tumbarumba and Griffith papers [with disappointing results], discussion with Wagga's most successful dance promotions operator during the time, photos, newspaper articles, advertised gigs and Rod Finlayson's diaries for part of 1966, all of 1967 and part of 1969. It would have been a massive boost both in memories and identified gigs played had he been able to find his diaries for 1968 and the rest of 1969. Pat Geaghan also kept gig diaries as he handled the bookings for The Mystics from late 1967, and subsequently Collection, but he thinks they were discarded during house removals years ago. Whilst I handled the bookings generally from the start as a lot of early gigs came through my mother who was on the Swimming Pool fund raising committee, I kept no information re gigs. I don't recall running a gig diary and can't remember how I kept track of where the band was booked - I must have had some system for recording gigs as we never failed to show up! Some licence has been used with a very small amount of information simply because exact details of actual gigs and/or events could not be determined or specifically remembered however, assumptions have been made e.g....all bands worked on New Year's Eve!

Where there is any doubt, a "[?]" appears next to the gig or the date of the gig in the Gig Guide – this indicates uncertainty in relation to the actual date or month of the gig or possibly the year. Notwithstanding that these gigs are ones where no advertised evidence or diary entries were found, there is no doubt about the gigs taking place. As an example, both bands played at Batchelor & Spinster [B&S] type balls or functions where the organisers and attendees considered themselves to generally come from "the professions, landed gentry or the perceived upper levels of society". These were never advertised as attendance was by invitation only thus ensuring that "riff-raff" would not drag down the level of social decorum the organisers and attendees liked to think their station in life deserved!

As well, some papers varied the size of their ads for dances – most dances were advertised in the Entertainment Section of the Classified Advertisements section of the respective papers with a huge "DANCE" or similar heading to catch the reader's attention however, others were very small ads without any special eye-catching print. This may have been the reason why gigs for some dance venues, where I know The Mystics or Collection played, have not been found in papers – the ads were simply missed because they were small and/or not in the usual section of the paper. This was evidenced by a re-scan of a Lockhart newspaper which revealed a couple of small ads in an unrelated section of the Classifieds, which had been previously missed. It was easier with The Wagga Daily Advertiser as it always placed dance ads on the last two pages of the paper - The Advertiser never contained an Entertainment section in the Classifieds, which all other smaller town papers did.

As some of the members continued on playing in other bands after The Mystics and Collection finished, this caused, at times, some confusion with gig and event information because the lapse of time has muddied the waters in terms of whether a certain gig or venue was played by the bands in this story, or subsequent bands the members were playing in. In some instances, special event gigs were held year after year for many years and subsequent bands with former Collection members, played these gigs thus also leading to some doubt either way.

Under the guise of "author's licence", I have included limited information relating to me personally which is to be taken purely as incidental information relative to the timeline of the two bands histories and because this story is written from my perspective as being the only band member who was in both bands from the beginning in 1965 until I left at the end of 1969 and The Rock connection ceased. In saying that, I have already acknowledged the other band members in compiling information. Understandably, whilst this is a storied history of the bands and the members as it relates to band gigs, events, incidents and happenings, not everything about the band members has been included, even if remembered! Some things need to be left undisturbed, unrevealed and the innocent protected! To add some additional local flavour, nicknames, as shown in the Band Member's Guide, have been used throughout the story.

I believe that the bulk of what is written is true, allowing for the passage of time and the reliability of memories – and anyhow, if you are reading this and for some reason you find an inconsistency or error in any of the following, it's now too late to make changes - to this edition. I would however appreciate being advised of any information which alters or adds to anything written herein, or, if suddenly someone becomes aware of or has never-before-seen photos in an old photo album, so that, in the unlikely event that demand requires a further edition to be printed, the updated information and/or photos can be included!

Peter Brown
Email: peterb48@outlook.com

The Bass Player 1969

In memory of my mother, **Nancy May Brown,** who was born at The Rock, and was a proudly involved and committed community member for 73 of her 93 years. She wholeheartedly supported my musical ambitions.

Publications researched

Wagga Daily Advertiser, Lockhart Review and Urana Advertiser, Eastern Riverina Chronicle, Tumbarumba Times, Temora Tribune, Junee Southern Cross, Tumut and Adelong Times and the Area News and associated publications.

Band Member's Guide

No Name   November 1965 – December 1965
                                       Les Magrath   Lead Guitar

Band	Dates	Member	Role
No Name	November 1965 – December 1965	Les Magrath	Lead Guitar
		Dennis McGrath [Porky]	Rhythm Guitar
		Peter Brown [Brownie]	Bass Guitar
		John Klimpsch [Charlie]	Drums
The GTs/The Mystics	December 1965 – February 1966	Col Moore [Seymour]	Vocals
		Des Condon	Lead Guitar
		Les Magrath	Rhythm Guitar
		Peter Brown	Bass Guitar
		Dennis McGrath	Drums
The Mystics [b]	February 1966 – September 1967	Col Moore	Vocals
		Rod Finlayson [Woody]	Lead
		Les Magrath	Rhythm
		Peter Brown	Bass
		Dennis McGrath	Drums
The Mystics [c]	September 1967 – November 1967	Col Moore	Vocals
		Pat Geaghan	Lead
		Les Magrath	Rhythm
		Peter Brown	Bass
		Dennis McGrath	Drums
The Mystics [d]	November 1967 – April 1968	Col Moore	Vocals
		Pat Geaghan	Lead
		Rod Finlayson	Rhythm
		Peter Brown	Bass
		Dennis McGrath	Drums
The Mystics [e]	May 1968 – October 1968	Garry McKenzie [Jock]	Vocals
		Pat Geaghan	Lead
		Rod Finlayson	Rhythm
		Peter Brown	Bass
		Robert Kitney [Dick]	Drums

The Mystics reformed and renamed Collection

        <u>October 1968 – December 1968</u>
Col Moore	Vocals
Pat Geaghan	Lead
Rod Finlayson	Rhythm
Peter Brown	Bass
Dennis McGrath	Drums

Collection [b]   <u>December 1968 – December 1969</u>
Col Moses [Uncle Col - Unc]	Vocals
Pat Geaghan	Lead
Rod Finlayson	Rhythm
Peter Brown	Bass
Dennis McGrath	Drums

Member's Time in Bands

Des Condon*	2 months	Dick Kitney*	6 months
Jock McKenzie	7 Months	Col Moses	12 months
Les Magrath *	24 months	Pat Geaghan	27 months
Col Moore	33 months	Dennis McGrath	43 months
Rod Finlayson	45 months	Peter Brown	49 months

From:

*The Rock   *Yerong Creek   *Wagga Wagga

Special Extras

2005 Reunion	David Wall	Keyboards
2007 Reunion	David Wall	Keyboards
	Nicholas "Nick" Freeman	Drums

Pre-1965

When did it all start?

My first recollections of taking any notice of music or even showing any interest in music could be traced back to listening to jazz records on a radiogram at my Auntie's house in The Rock probably around the age of 10 or 11 i.e. the very late 1950's and beginning of the 1960s. The one record I remember from this time was the Graeme Bell Jazz Band's "Rag Trade" album – I can still see the cover of the album in my mind's eye! I also remember listening to Wagga radio station 2WG before mum and dad got up of a morning, sitting in a big old lounge chair in our lounge room and banging away keeping beat with my fists on one of the arms of the chair to songs that were being played on the radio – the driving back beat of Johnny and the Hurricanes "Red River Rock" was an early catalyst for me being drawn into a lifelong involvement in modern music!

In 1961, I was sent off to boarding school at St Paul's College, Walla Walla, a small southern NSW town with a German heritage and the largest Lutheran Church, after completing primary school at The Rock Central School. In my second or third year there, one of the boarders had an acoustic guitar and I started to take an interest in it although I can't remember if as a result, I learnt chords or was simply mucking about with it. Whatever, the guitar had something about it which interested me.

Me, aged about 14, at boarding school with the borrowed guitar. Not too sure about the chord formation or how the guitar strap should be worn!

The idea of forming a band arose out of Dennis "Porky" McGrath and me listening to records by The Shadows in the early 1960's. This would have been when I was home from boarding school on holidays or long weekend exeats. We would use tennis racquets as pretend guitars and mime to The Shadows Greatest Hits LP, which I played on a small red plastic record player with a very tinny sound - our favourite number was Apache - I think most aspiring guitar players of that era [post-war baby boomers] would agree, The Shadows were a massive influence on future guitar players. I can distinctly remember miming our pretend band to Shadows numbers at Marty Ward's place in the main street of The Rock and the Verdon's house in Urana Street. Even though I was pretending to play a tennis racquet "guitar", my main musical interest had changed to the drums. Tony Meehan, The Shadows drummer, was my inspiration.

At boarding school, I remember being in a pretend band in an end of term concert when I was in 3rd Year, where we mimed to Elvis and Cliff Richard records - I played the "drums" made up of tin food cans of various sizes I got from the kitchen maids in the school dining room which were stuck on wooden sticks and the others had various forms of pretend guitars such as tennis racquets and large T-squares, which were used as blackboard rulers, and the like – an early version of an "air guitar". To add a visual effect, we hung a sheet in front of the stage and had a spotlight shining on us from the back of the stage which projected shadows of the "band" onto the sheet – we got a lot of good comments about the whole effect.

During this time, I applied to learn piano and do music as a subject. I went to the music teacher for an audition and her way of determining who took up lessons and who didn't was based on how well you could sing a musical scale. Not being a singer, I didn't pass the test and so didn't get accepted for piano – I wonder how many famous piano players couldn't sing? Bafflingly, the music teacher picked me to become one of the three bass section singers in the school choir and I can recall her comment one day at choir practice that our voices blended so well – the other two must have been pretty good! This early setback did not dent my interest in music. Another baffling decision was that I was chosen to play The Judge [one of the main characters] in Trial by Jury, a Gilbert and Sullivan operetta, for a school concert – not bad for someone who couldn't sing, although this didn't necessarily mean I could – maybe no-one else wanted the part!

In 1964 both Les and Porky went to Sydney for the year to do their PMG [Post-Master General, subsequently Telstra] technician's training. They were in Sydney when Billy Thorpe and the Aztecs and Ray Brown and the Whispers were making a name for themselves at Surf City and The Easybeats were already on the rise as a top group. When they came home at the end of the year, Porky told us about going to see these bands and Les had a pair of the latest Beatle boots, which were all the rage in Sydney.

In 1965 both Les and Porky had finished their training and were back in Wagga working with the PMG and I was in my last year at boarding school. I distinctly remember receiving a phone call from Porky one afternoon late in the year telling me that Les and he had bought guitars and Les had also bought an amp and that they were forming a band. I volunteered to be the drummer, but Porky said John "Charlie" Klimpsch had a set and he would fill that role but what they needed was a bass player, so I happily agreed to change my instrument preference because I didn't want to miss out on the opportunity. Following this decision, drawn pictures of Fender basses started appearing throughout my school-work books and I had a drawing I did of Paul McCartney and his Beatle bass somewhere in my memorabilia – and I found it in an old shoebox with one last search whilst doing a final edit of this story!

My boarding school drawing of Paul McCartney and his Höfner bass – and Ringo!

When I finished boarding school and finally returned home in mid-November, we set about getting something happening musically - we were all either 16 or 17. In 1965, mum and dad had built a new house next door to our old house in Day Street and mum said that if I helped with the internal painting, she would buy me a bass guitar in payment - which I did and which she did – the bass cost $25 and was purchased from Stan Jones' Harmony House music shop in Wagga.

Around this time, I went to a dance at The Rock Hall and The Corvettes, a popular Wagga band at the time, were playing. At the end of the night I went up and spoke with Ian Price, their bass player and asked if I could have a look at his Fender Jazz Bass – he said I could even pick it up and I remember that I was shaking like a leaf as I got it out of its case on the stage – the excitement of holding that Fender Jazz was so intense that I went home that night and couldn't get to sleep – the adrenalin of holding the best bass ever made had me totally pumped up.

On another occasion, the Roberts Brothers, Dave and Bernard, from Mangoplah, were playing at a dance at the hall, and Bernard was playing a bright lime green double cut away semi acoustic electric bass – to me, it was stunning!

Now that we had three guitars and a drum kit, our first practices were held in the Methodist Church Hall across the street from the school at The Rock. Dot Magrath, Les's mother, arranged this for us through the church. The few residents who lived near the hall along Bourke's Creek used to complain that the noise upset their TV reception but there was never any real drama. Some of the local kids would turn up and stand outside listening - none of us really understood music or chords or bass parts, although I think Les had worked out basic E, A and D chords, and I don't think Charlie knew too much about drumming either – he had learnt piano. Les, Porky and I all played through Les's little grey Maton amp. Les had purchased the sheet music for Apache and it was the first tune we attempted to play – Les playing lead guitar and Porky on rhythm guitar [not knowing how to play any chords] and me with hardly any knowledge of bass playing. Musically, it must have sounded terrible, but not to us! I had one photo of this group practicing in the hall for years but now can't locate it! These practices did not last very long!

The GT's

In early December 1965, Porky was on Christmas leave from the PMG and went to work helping with the wheat harvest at Condon's farm, which was on the Mangoplah Road at Yerong Creek. There he met Des Condon, who was about the same age as us, who could play guitar, and who also owned a set of drums. Porky rang me and Les and we were invited down to the farm to have a practice with Des – Charlie was left off the invitation because Porky had been mucking around on Des's drums and had decided he preferred the drums over a guitar. Des had a no-name solid body double cutaway guitar he had purchased from Stan Jones and a small 15watt amp his dad had bought him. He was much more advanced than Les and I musically and consequently was able to show Les chords and he helped me to understand how the bass worked around the chords. Porky seemed to take to the drums very quickly, so Charlie was out before he was actually in. This very first "practice" was held inside the house, but future practices were in their woolshed. I think we initially started to learn a couple of instrumental tunes, however, the big thing on the radio were The Beatles and other British groups. We decided that, despite our deference to The Shadows, it was now 1965, not 1961, and being a guitar instrumental band was no-longer the way to go and the band needed a singer - I suggested Col "Seymour" Moore, my best mate, as I had often heard him singing when I stayed with him out on his family farm and thought he had a good voice. Seymour came down with Les and I the next time we had a rehearsal and after a few practices, we managed to be able to belt out a couple of songs, probably not all that well – but it was an advance on a start! As we were now unofficially a band, we needed a name and I distinctly remember Porky thinking up the name, "The GT's", although none of us was really into hot cars. Porky formed the name on the bass drum front skin using black adhesive tape – a big G and a big T! The name didn't last long!

Name Change to The Mystics

The change of name and who thought of it, is totally lost to history, however, someone came up with "The Mystics" and it was a name we liked - Des clearly remembers playing gigs as The Mystics from day one. The name, The GTs didn't get much further than being on the front of Des's drums in the woolshed at Condon's – it certainly did not make it onto any stage.

First Gig – Freebie

The band continued to practice and rehearse songs a couple of times a week in the Condon's woolshed - we looked forward to the practices because we could see we were starting to get somewhere.

The news that we had something happening reached some Collingullie girls who had been at school at The Rock with us when we were in primary school. They rang and asked if we could play at a dance on a Sunday night at the Collingullie Hall. I think this would have been just prior to Christmas 1965. We agreed to do the gig and I remember we thought we had hit the big-time – our first gig was a freebie, which didn't matter to us! This first ever gig was held outside, rather than inside, at the rear of the hall. There was no temporary stage for the band, so we simply set up our gear on the ground next to the rear entry stairs onto the back of the stage and the punters danced in the dirt and dust. The reason we were outside most likely was that it was a hot night and the tin hall would have been like an oven inside.

As we hadn't been going very long, we didn't know very many songs so on that night at Collingullie, we kept repeating the few songs we had learnt over and over to fill in the couple of hours that we were asked to play – as it was a freebie I don't think the punters were too concerned with the very short song list. Des recalls that we did the Dave Clark 5's "Glad all over" [he reckons a big hit with the punters] and Normie Rowe's "Shakin' all over" and according to Des, they were very responsive because we were playing popular songs off the radio. Another song was The Yardbirds "For your love" which was Des's favourite! I think we also did Normie Rowe's other hit, "It ain't necessarily so", although this might have been added later as our song list grew. All very ambitious for a band just starting out.

During the night, somebody accidentally knocked Les's guitar over while it was leaning against his amp during a break, and the neck cracked where it joined the guitar body, which was neither a good start for Les nor the band! Something also happened to Porky's father's car which he had borrowed to get the drums to the gig at Collingullie – it boiled going up Ryan's Hill, just out of The Rock [which supports that it was a hot day] and Porky had to stop and wait for the engine to cool. He made sure the radiator was full before we headed home after the gig.

There is no memory of this very first gig's aftermath but without any doubt, we would have all got together the next day to recap the night and highlight the triumphs [which in our eyes would have been many despite the short song list] and there would have been much excitement and expectation about what was ahead for The Mystics in 1966.

1966

In late 1965 after leaving boarding school, I had started work at the Southern Riverina County Council in Wagga and was put under the guidance of a slightly older young bloke called Terry Stirzaker, who just happened to play bass for The Shantines, Wagga's best band at that time - I couldn't believe my luck! Terry was a great bass player and because I was a fellow bass player, albeit still learning at the time, we had a common interest to distract us. At times, when we were supposed to be working for the SRCC, Terry would be drawing bass guitar fretboards on the desk blotter and showing me where the notes were and how to play bass patterns – at times, work became secondary to both of us! We have stayed in contact and remained friends ever since.

Foot in mouth – twice!

I was with Terry and a couple of his fellow band mates from The Shantines having a sandwich lunch at the Memorial Gardens in Fitzmaurice Street one lunchtime – we were sitting on the lawn in the gardens and Terry and the others waved to a couple of fairly solid girls who were walking past on the footpath. I asked Terry who they were, and he said, "A couple of fans!" to which I responded, "At that size, you'd only need one to make up a fan club!" I thought my comment was very funny until Terry said that one of them was his sister! – one foot in!

It could well have been that very same day – the discussion was obviously around music and I made the [in]famous statement from my very limited musical knowledge at that time that, with a guitar in mind, there was no lower chord than E – they just fell about laughing so I demonstrated by using my right arm as a guitar arm, and forming an E chord with the fingers of my left hand in the approximate E position near my right wrist [which represented the headstock], to prove my point – "See, you can't get any lower than an E chord on the guitar arm!" - that only cut them up more! Then one of them pointed out to me that D, C, B, A, G and F are all lower than E because of the cyclical nature of musical notes! After a little thought, the penny dropped, so I pushed the other foot in as well!

First Paid Gigs

The Shantines had a regular 50/50 Saturday night gig at the Police Boys Club with the Riverina Jazz Band. The Jazz Band usually had a break after Christmas, and as I was working with Terry at the time, he kindly arranged for The Mystics to be booked as replacements for the Jazz Band and we played 50/50 with The Shantines over two Saturday night dances in January. This was a pretty gutsy effort by Terry because we had only been going a matter of weeks and our song list and our musical talents would have been both very limited. Notwithstanding, I think we got paid £5 each – we felt like millionaires - it was quite a while before we started earning this amount regularly for gigs. None of the band who were working, was earning any more than about £15-20 a week at their day job so to go out and play for a couple of hours and get a quarter of what we earned all week, was almost unbelievable. I think we just managed to sound OK up against the best band in Wagga who gave us heaps of encouragement and best of all, Des recalls the punters danced when we played, which was a good sign of being accepted as a band and/or that the sound was OK. He remembers that we got a pretty good reception even though our song list was still very limited, and we again repeated songs and according to Des, quite a few people from both The Rock and Yerong Creek were there to see the band perform professionally for the first time. A point of interest is that the rhythm player with The Shantines was Pat Geaghan, who was basically unknown to us then, but who will feature later in this story.

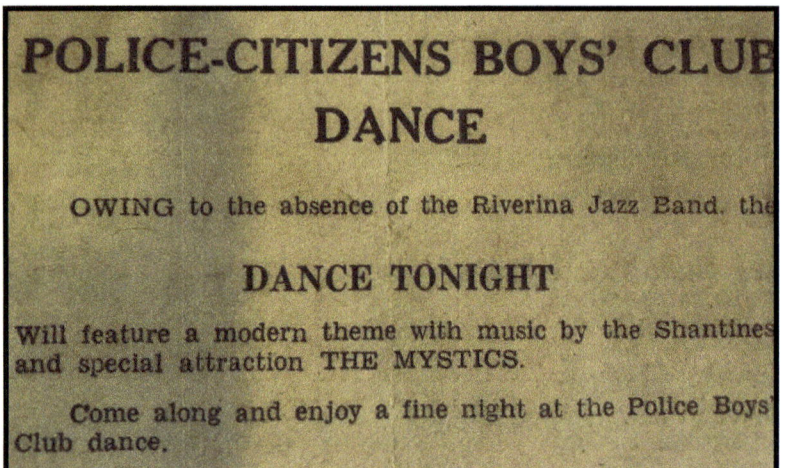

Despite not finding an ad for our very first gig when I researched the Wagga Daily Advertiser and being disappointed that our first professional gig went un-announced, as I was editing this whole story for the last time, I had one final look in my music room at home for anything to do with the band and came across this in an old shoebox.

The Mystics first professional gig

My initial story line had lamented why the Boys Club did not advertise dances and the reason was that everyone knew that they ran dances every week, or every two weeks and that advertising was unnecessary. Well, they advertised us and that's all that matters! This was the start of four fantastic years. It is interesting to note that we were playing a paid gig within about 6 weeks of forming the band despite having a very limited song list. After one of these gigs, Les says that we delivered him to the Wagga Railway station so he could catch the train to Sydney at midnight as he had to undergo a refresher week at the PMG training facility.

After I received my Leaving Certificate marks in mid-January, which revealed a "Fail" and just how little study I did for the my final Leaving exams at boarding school, I decided go back to school, but this time to Wagga High, so when school commenced for 1966 in late January, I resigned from the job, and reluctantly, from Terry's free bass tuition classes.

Following are a couple of early photos taken at Les's place probably early 1966 – they are obviously taken on the same day. I appear to have thought better of having photos taken with my new second-hand bass in shorts so must have raced home and changed into long pants and grabbed a coat. The hats belonged to Jock, Les's dad! My new second-hand amp is in the background along with Les's amp which copped a real hiding when three of us were going through it in the Methodist Hall. From the shape, our guitars appear to be both Coronas. Les was on his third guitar by this time and the band had only been going a couple of months. These photos were most likely taken by one of Les's sisters. His guitar in the photo did not last long because the neck warped.

First Gig at The Rock Hall

Whilst this gig in our hometown should have been a milestone gig also, there was no paper ad to announce this major event in the band's progress and none of the band except Des can remember this at all, but it must have been for the Swimming Pool Committee and mum would have booked us. The only thing I can recall about our first gig at The Rock was that Lyn and Cheryl Tinnock raved about how good the band was when we saw them down the street the next day – we probably weren't that flash but being local it wouldn't have mattered how we sounded – we were immediately local heroes.

Two cool cats – Les in his Beatle boots – then Les in no Beatle boots!
Me in shorts – then me in no shorts! If only we could play something!

Des says he can remember this was the only gig he did with the band at The Rock and that he thinks it was to let everybody know that the band was up and running! He remembers that we drew a terrific crowd and one of the fans from Uranquinty showed great enthusiasm towards him as he was leaving the hall after the dance!

St John's Hall

Les remembers an early gig [no gig ad found] at St John's Hall, Wagga, with Des still in the band and although Des's memory is very hazy, he did confirm that he played at the hall, which if correct, places the gig in late January or early February. More particularly, the reason Les remembers this gig is that there was not a very big crowd but among the punters were a group of RAAF apprentices [known as "Sprogs" in those days] and whoever was running the dance took the microphone to castigate the girls for refusing to dance with the RAAF blokes "…..who would one day be defending our country"! This negative attitude by girls towards RAAF apprentices and Army recruits at dances was common in those days and they were often a target of local young blokes outside the dances, and fights were a regular part of dance nights.

Band Change

The band continued to rehearse at Condon's, and from memory, usually on a Saturday or Sunday afternoon. I didn't have a car so I would normally travel down with Les who often borrowed his father's EJ Holden. On one occasion, the car was not available so Les had to borrow his dad's International 4-ton hay carting truck. It must have been a sight – two young blokes in a big truck with amps and guitars roped onto the back tray, doing about 40 miles an hour down the highway to Yerong Creek – much the same as the early Beatles who often used buses to get themselves and their gear to gigs!

The band had been going for only a couple of months into 1966. It was in February and my memory was that Des did not want to continue with the band, his reason being that he was more into the

Blues and he could see we were keen on the straight pop stuff – an apparent early musical difference! However, Des says it was because he was moving to Wagga for an apprenticeship and he couldn't see himself driving out to The Rock for practices. Des believes that he did only four gigs with the band although Les remembers the extra gig with Des in the band at St Johns in Wagga. Des says that he had already had discussions with Garry "Jock" McKenzie about forming a band in Wagga [he will come into the story later] – they had been at boarding school together at Albury Grammar, as had Seymour. They had started a shared interest in music as Des had his guitar at school and Jock played a set of drums that belonged to the school. According to Jock, Des said when he moved to Wagga from the farm, he wanted to form a band and that he would teach Jock bass and they would get a drummer and organ player to make up the new group. As it turned out, Des joined a band called Lost and Found when he moved to Wagga and stayed in the band for the rest of the year and only left to join Jock at the end of 1966.

To Des's credit, rather than just leave us a guitarist short when we had only just begun, he had a mate in Yerong Creek, Rod "Woody" Finlayson, who he invited along to a practice. Even at this early stage of the band's existence, I recall we were not too keen on accepting a new member into the band, but we had no other option. We soon got over our concern when it became apparent that Woody was a good guitarist and would be a good replacement for Des, he knew songs that suited us, and he could sing harmony. Des's departure meant we had to find a new practice place and Seymour's farm woolshed at The Rock was the only place available, even if it was at times, full of sheep waiting to be shorn. Later, we started to also use The Rock Hall on a Saturday afternoon when playing there that night and that often caused the local kids to call in and listen whilst we worked out and rehearsed new songs.

First Instruments

Following the damage to Les's original guitar, which was a semi-acoustic single cutaway Sunburst Eko, he decided to make his own guitar. "Dutchy" Van Ree had made a guitar body when he was at school but didn't do anything with it – Les got the guitar body from Dutchy and used the neck and fittings from the Eko to complete his homemade blended model which needed the grip of Tarzan when playing bar chords. The guitar body was modelled on a Maton Firebird and in Les's own words, it was never much good. He bought another guitar, a Corona, from Stan Jones but the neck warped not long after, so on a refresher training trip back to Sydney, he saw a Maton Flamingo in a pawn shop in Parramatta and bought it for $25 – he then had it resprayed from the original cherry red/pink to sky blue – he reckons Terry Stirzaker offered to buy it from him at the 2005 reunion concert as it was a very rare Maton model.

As Porky had been using Des's small drum kit, which would no longer be available to him, he bought his first kit from Stan Jones's music shop as well. It was a set of Black Diamond Remos – snare, single mounted tom, floor tom and bass drum with ride and crash cymbals and a set of hi-hats - he carried all the fittings around in an old suitcase. It was a very big day for the band when Porky turned up to practice with "The Mystics" painted on the bass drum skin – we were now officially a band, and everyone would know who we were.

The original "The Mystics" on Porky's Bass drum

Woody played a Suttons solid body double cutaway guitar through a little amp and I had a Conora solid body bass [I believe Terry Stirzaker may have owned the bass until he traded it to buy a Fender

Jazz], which I played through a blonde Moody 60 watt bass amp I brought from Frank Davey, who had been in an early band with Jacky McGrath [pre-Shantines] - he originally played a Tea-chest bass. Seymour purchased a PA system consisting of a PA head and two small columns plus three small mics with stands, from Pitmans store in Wagga. I remember the mics were very small and probably not suitable for singing but we used them for a while until it became apparent that proper vocal mikes were available and much better.

The Rock Hall Dances

A committee had been formed to raise money to build a community swimming pool at The Rock. The committee was made up of parents including my mother, Nancy, plus a small band of volunteers which included Les Molkentin. Les should have been given a medal as he nearly always collected the entry money at the door and also acted in a security capacity to ensure there was no trouble inside the hall, and for most of the night, copped the sound of the band bouncing off the back wall behind him – but he never complained. I think Frank McGrath also was involved in some capacity with the dances.

The Mystics gave the committee an opportunity to raise money by running regular dances in the hall at The Rock and in return, it gave the band an opportunity to get experience and pick up some extra spending money. The dances seem to have been held almost every two weeks, were popular and very successful from the beginning, and kids came from all over the district. It was a novelty for the kids from The Rock to see a bunch of local boys, who played in the local footy side, up on the stage. There was never any alcohol in the hall but there was in the boot of cars parked out the front of the hall, and the blokes would disappear between brackets. At one of these early dances, I remember wearing my old boarding school uniform one night [a blazer, school shirt and tie, and short pants], just as a laugh – Angus Young of AC/DC made this his trademark uniform, but I was about 8 years ahead of him.

Unfortunately, dances for the Swimming Pool Committee at The Rock were not advertised in the Lockhart, Henty or Wagga papers however there is no doubt that the band played all the Swimming Pool Committee's fund-raising dances in the first two years and always drew a crowd. Later dances at The Rock were by the RSL Auxiliary Committee and the YCW after the Swimming Pool Committee ceased running dances around early 1968. Because we rehearsed in the hall during the afternoon before a dance, after Pat joined the band, he can remember that Mum would sometimes bring sandwiches up to the hall for us. Woody was a notoriously late sleeper, so we did a bit of waiting around for him to turn up from Yerong Creek. There were times when the rest of us where ready to start practice. But Woody was missing. Someone would have to go to a phone [no convenient mobiles around then] and ring Woody's place and his mother would tell us that he had just got up and as soon as he has had something to eat, he would be on his way! They say patience is a virtue, but it can be a pain in the arse too!

Early songs

Apart from those already mentioned earlier, the following is a very small list of other songs we did – "Do the Hanky Panky" [cheesy but popular], "Let it be me", "House of the Rising Sun", and "Summertime". We always ended the night with "500 Miles", a Seymour favourite, which he is still requested to sing – a slow number that allowed couples to dance close for the last dance before heading off home or elsewhere!!! Even Porky got into the action by singing "As tears go by" [occasionally], a Stones song, while Seymour held the mike to Porky's mouth [no spare mike stands at this early stage]. Porky was the only Stones fan in the band consequently The Mystics never did any other Stones songs. Other songs from this time were,

"The Snoopy Song" [a comedy number], "And I love her", "Eight Days a week" and "No reply" by The Beatles, "Congratulations" and "I could easily fall" by Cliff Richard, "No milk today", "I'm Henry the 8th", and "A Kind of a Hush" by Herman's Hermits, "Little Red Riding Hood" by Sam the Sham and The Pharaohs, "She's so fine" and "Wedding Ring" by The Easybeats and the two tempo number, "Stepping Stone", by The Monkeys. A song that really got the crowd [and the band] going was "Gloria" by Them – we could hear the punters singing along over the loudness of the amps and drums.

Another song that was a favourite of the punters had only three words. It was a number by Billy Thorpe and the Aztecs, and the entire song consisted of the words - "Mashed potato, yeah!", sung to a 12 bar blues pattern - probably in E, the key for any 12-bar song in those days! I think it required all the front line to jump every time the word "Yeah" was sung. Seymour would get the punters going and the crowd would be rocking and singing along – it always ended with plenty of approval and applause.

As has been the case with other recollections for this story, remembering songs and when we played them has been misted by the 50+ years since they were played. Some numbers which were recalled as being part of the song list in the early years, on investigation, related to a later period of the band. Few of the songs in the first two years were musically very challenging, not that our musical ability at this stage allowed us to be very adventurous - we played songs that were hits and popular at the time but with a limited number of chords. The only standout from this was The Yardbirds "For your love" because it was bluesy rather than popular, and which I believe was the very first song we learned with Des Condon. Whilst the Reunion song list at the end of this story contains many of the songs we used to do, there are many more that have not been included.

First Lockhart Gig

The band was booked to play its first gig in Lockhart in the Supper Room of the Lockhart Memorial Hall on the 9th April. Interestingly, the band was advertised as "The Rock Orchestra" which probably indicates the age of the person placing the ad in the local paper, and the possibility that after booking the band, they forgot the band's name – a probability as we were still establishing ourselves. Clearly it was The Mystics because the only other band that did some work in Lockhart, and came from The Rock, was Bert Pertzel's Old Time Band [The Foot Tappers] and they never did any dances in the Supper Room where the teenage dances were held. Porky nicknamed Bert's band, "Bert and the Bladder Boys"! Bert had a disability in his right leg, the leg he used for his bass drum pedal, and to get the leg working, Bert used a partially inflated Aussie Rules football bladder to, once started, keep his leg bouncing up and down on the pedal! What a technique!

We continued to practice as much as we could to get more songs onto the song list, and as well, learnt a bracket of instrumentals which we would play at the beginning of gigs because it usually took a little while for the crowd to build up and we didn't want to waste songs on the few early punters.

> ROD FINLAYSON: *"Where art thou, Julie?"* A Cadet C.U.O., he is also interested in Cricket, Rugby League and Australian Rules. Outside school he is the Lead Guitarist of a quite well known band.

> PETER BROWN: "Thou shag eared rebel." TR-YC A.R.F.C. player. Athletic champ. Plays bass for Mystics despite football knuckles. Now knows the difference between 13 and 18.

Work and Football

With Woody and I on the school bus to Wagga High School every day, it was a great time to discuss new songs, chords, gigs, and girls.

Woody's and my Wagga High School Year-Book entries for 1966. The band's reputation was spreading!

Both Porky and Les worked for the PMG. Porky had been transferred to Griffith in early 1966 for a few months and then on to Jerilderie – Les was working in Wagga. Porky travelled home from Jerilderie weekends to play and rehearse. During the footy season, Les, Seymour and I played 1st grade for The Rock-Yerong Creek Australian Football Club. Porky was playing 1st Grade football at Jerilderie. The band was not working every week at this stage but still managed to play a number of gigs each month, mainly at The Rock, Lockhart and Collingullie – at times, Porky would drive home after playing footy for Jerilderie to do a Saturday night gig. He said he often got questions as to why his drum kit was in the car when he turned up at the gate to whatever ground Jerilderie were playing footy at and he had to explain that he would be heading straight home for a gig after playing – consequently, he was always asked what band he was in.

I can't remember who worked out the chords to songs, but most likely Woody had assumed this role with maybe some help from me. We worked up new songs each practice to add to the song list as well as some old-time stuff for the barn dance and this would be enough to get us through a gig. I think that we sometimes purchased sheet music for songs – continually replacing the needle on a record so that we could work out chords and words was always a very time-consuming way of learning songs and I am sure this added to our learning experience. – it taught us to listen and concentrate closely on what was being played and sung.

The Supper Room at Lockhart Memorial Hall – a regular venue for The Mystics

A Tragedy

The band had a gig at The Rock Hall on Easter Thursday, and a girl Porky had met whilst he was doing his training in Sydney the previous year, was coming down for the Easter break. I think this was the very first time she had ever been out of Sydney but tragically there was a car accident and she was killed. Porky kept in contact with her mother for a while, but these contacts were always very stressful for both.

The Band Gig Posters

Julie McGrath, Porky's sister who was only 12 years old when the band started, used to make up posters for dances that were held at The Rock, and as well, for any other town that was close by. To get news of dances at The Rock to other towns, local people would take Julie's posters to put up in a local café if they were heading to or passing through Henty or Culcairn or going out to Collingullie or Lockhart. I think she started using the wording "The Mighty Mystics" in the posters which was a cool alternative name. This extension of the name would appear later in paper ads for dances in Wagga.

After the Gig

Sometimes after gigs at The Rock, after packing up our gear, we would head out the Old Wagga Road, light a fire and stand around having a drink. From memory, we usually drank beer from large cans but occasionally the drink was a bottle of Porphyry Pearl, because it was cheap – probably the worst wine ever made. I can also remember Marsala [a fortified wine] being a drink that was sometimes an alternative. Les turned 18 early in the year but Porky and I were still 17, and Seymour and Woody were 16 so most of us were under the legal age to be drinking.

The Pops Bucket

Between brackets at The Rock Hall, we would be in the dressing room behind the stage, which was the old projection room when the hall used to be used as a picture theatre. There was always a bucket full of "pops", stuff to put on the floorboards in the hall so the dancers could slide when doing old time dances where sliding was part of the dance – it was very similar to fine sawdust. I think Porky started pissing in the pops bucket because he couldn't be bothered going down to the old toilets at the rear of the hall yard - and we all followed suit. Someone would come up and get the pops bucket at some stage during the night [probably before the barn dance] and then scatter the pops all around the hall floor – surprisingly, nobody ever complained of the smell or that the sawdust might have been a bit damp!

Kyeamba Smith Hall, Wagga Showgrounds

This dance venue started up in about July 1966 and The Shantines were the regular band managed by Keith Bird who operated After 5 Promotions which ran the dances and booked bands from Melbourne, Sydney and Adelaide. It was not until December 1967 that The Mystics were booked for the first time to appear at this big dance venue with a top Aussie singer **[see 1967]**. We did, however, go to dances at the showground when we didn't have a gig because the top recording bands played there and I remember going to the showgrounds to see The Masters Apprentices, MPD Ltd and The Twilights.

Gigs and Gig Bookings

It is impossible to provide any commentary on gigs for 1966 as apart from the small number identified early in the year, the rest of the year is a blank in respect to venues and who the gigs were for [see Woody's Gig Diary]. The first lot of gigs in the year were all gigs from our collective memories except the one at Lockhart where the ad in the Lockhart paper described the featured band as "The Rock Orchestra"! I suppose our early gig at Lockhart must have impressed the locals [or the organisers] enough to re-book the band. It is impossible to identify other gig venues, but is would be safe to say that the band played at The Rock for the Swimming Pool Committee every two weeks as well as Collingullie, Lockhart and an odd night at Yerong Creek would have been the main venues. Henty did not become a regular gig for the band until after June 1967 when the band played its first advertised gig at the Memorial Hall.

From memory, I got the job of handling the bookings basically because mum organised the dance bookings for the Swimming Pool Committee. I can vaguely remember getting phone calls at home re gigs elsewhere. We didn't advertise who handled the bookings so people wanting to book the band simply rang The Rock Telephone Exchange [town population at that time about 500] which was part of The Rock Post Office and which was manned 24 hours a day by switchboard telephonists. The caller simply requested to be connected to whoever handled the bookings for The Mystics. The Rock dances gave us plenty of exposure, and bookings for dances in towns around The Rock, continued to come in.

Porky Missing

The band only ever did one gig at Uranquinty and the date is buried in the mists of time – it was in the local hall and Porky was unavailable for reasons also forgotten. The rest of the band decided we would get Ray Charters, a drummer [and in our opinion, a person who was very confident with his own ability], from Wagga to fill in. Ray was a reasonable drummer, tended to be a bit showy and had a different style to what we were used to. The gig was a bit of a struggle and after it was over, we took a decision never to use any other drummer again. Porky was unusual because he was left-handed, and his kit was setup accordingly and I don't recall any other drummer around at the time being left-handed. He was a good basic and consistent drummer, and like the rest of us, was still learning. Obviously, his style suited the band because he was developing his style as the band was developing its overall style and sound. Porky was very much the same as Ringo with the Beatles – not noted for drum solos but for a solid and consistent rhythm section back beat.

The band regularly played at Lockhart in the Supper Room of the RSL Hall in the main street. One night, Les played a song whilst lying flat on his back – rather than it being some sort of "way out" stage show, it caused the rest of us, and the punters who gave him a wide berth, to wonder if he was on the same planet as the rest of us!

First Band Suits

During the year, as the band was starting to play gigs on a regular basis, a decision was taken to get a band uniform to complete the band look. We were simply copying the bands we liked, and it would also give the band a more professional appearance As I bought my casual clothes at Tony Quinlivan's

The Mystics in new blue corduroy suits at the Urana Hall
Back L to R: Seymour, Brownie, Les and Woody - Front: Porky
Unfortunately, this is one of only two photos of the band from this period.

Menswear in Wagga, I arranged for Tony to organise the suits, which were made from navy blue corduroy with pale blue shirts. For the first time, we looked like a band, but there is only one photo of The Mystics in the new suits and it was taken at the Urana Hall – in fact, apart from another photo taken by The Daily Advertiser, the suits photo is the only photo of the group while Les was in the band. Popular thinking is that the band wore the suits when playing at a Urana Footy Club premiership presentation function, but this is not correct. I found an ad for this function in the Lockhart Express, but another band is listed as being booked, so it remains a mystery as to what function The Mystics played for its only appearance at Urana in the new suits – there was certainly some connection to the local footy club so it could have been a dance organised for the night of grand-final day. I very vaguely remember posing for the photo on the stage of the Urana Hall and the photo certainly shows the band as being very young! The booking came through connections of Seymour who had relatives out there. The Urana gig would have been the longest trip the band had had to travel to play to this point and it is lost to time and memory as to what transport was used. Porky certainly had a car, Les and Seymour would have had access to family cars – Woody probably had his licence by then so was driving himself to The Rock to join the rest of us before we headed off.

New Guitars

Sometime during 1966, Woody and I decided to upgrade our instruments and purchased new guitars from Stan Jones at Harmony House. Woody bought an Elite ES-335 Style Hollow body Closet Classic, modelled on a Gibson 335, and my bass was the Elite Hollow body, modelled on a Gibson EB2. The manufacturer was an Italian company, Crucianelli, who were also well-known for making piano accordions – but they also sold a lot of guitars. They were great moderately priced guitars and produced a good sound. Woody owned two and still has one! I had mine for years until one of my daughters, when she was small, jumped on it whilst it was laying in its open guitar case, and severely cracked the beautiful sun-burst body – I subsequently sold it at a garage sale.

The Barn Dance

Dances in the early days, often required the band to play an old-time dance during the night and the most popular was the Barn Dance. It was a progressive group dance which required two circles of dancers – the inner circle, girls, and the outer circle, boys, with the boys remaining basically stationary with the girls progressively moving from one partner to the next on continuous rotation. The boys always thought it was a great way to chat up the girls as they got to dance with each girl as they progressed from partner to partner. There is an old joke about the boys hitting every girl up for sex later in the night as she passed in the rotation with the result that, whilst they got lots of negative responses, they also got a few positive ones!

Porky often liked to announce the barn dance by inviting everyone to -
a] "Sorm a fircle" [Form a Circle], or,
b] "…get in a ring!" This cracked us up every time but none of the punters ever got the joke! Towards the end of the year, the band was gaining popularity and dances at The Rock Hall still dragged in the crowds and the Swimming Pool Committee continued to do well financially.

The First Jerilderie Gig

As Porky was working for the PMG in Jerilderie, he used to travel home each weekend in his Mini whenever we had a gig or to rehearse. He had been telling all and sundry in Jerilderie about the band which eventually resulted in the band being booked to go over and play at a dance which was to be compered by a DJ from radio station 2QN in Deniliquin. The actual date remains a mystery, but it is believed to have been late in the year - Porky and Les confirm that the venue was the new Jerilderie Civic Hall and that we may have been the first band to appear there and Porky remembers balloons and streamers around the walls.

Despite popular opinion, the DJ was not Groover Wayne [see 1969] as research shows that he never worked for 2QN. The DJ [there is some conjecture as to whether he was actually from 2QN or 3SR Shepparton] had been giving us such a rap over the local radio station in the weeks and days leading up to the gig that the locals were totally fired up and the hall was absolutely packed for our appearance. We drove out there in two cars – Seymour's new Holden and Les in his father's EK - Porky probably stayed in Jerilderie and waited for us to arrive on the Saturday.

Les reckons that during the night, beers were being brought to us in the band room between brackets and that towards the end of the night I had started to show the affects. He remembers that I called the DJ a poofter [why, who knows?] which wasn't very smart considering the publicity he had given the band! Les can't remember if there was any response. Not exactly out of the "How to win friends and influence people" book!

The dance was a huge success and we went over very well. After the gig and we had packed up our gear, we were invited out to a property where a party was underway in a woolshed – one punter was so drunk he drank a glass of sheep dip so others at the party put him in a wool bale bag and tied it up so he couldn't do anymore damage to himself. We later crashed at a house in Jerilderie owned by Noel Maxwell, one of Porky's Jerilderie mates. Woody said he slept in a car owned by another Jerilderie local, Harry Winkler, and Les slept in his own car. I managed to score an old lounge chair in the loungeroom of the house for the night and clearly remember another bloke, who was also sleeping in another chair, getting up during the night and having a piss in the corner of the room and then flopping back into the chair and going back to sleep.

Greg Verdon [Verdo] says that he and Blue McGrath also went out to Jerilderie in Seymour's vehicle and remembers the events in the woolshed after the dance. They stayed at one of the pubs for the night. Carol [Molkentin] McGrath, Les's girlfriend at the time, said she and her sister Bev, also drove the 90 miles out to Jerilderie just to go to the dance and didn't get back to The Rock until around 3 am – a pretty gutsy effort for those days, late at night across the lonely Urana plains and no male passengers in case of an emergency!

The next morning, a kindly old lady from across the street asked us all over to her house for a cooked breakfast even though we would have kept her awake making a hell of a din in the late hours of the early morning until the party died and everyone crashed.

For some time, I had noticed an old double bass which was in Stan Jones' music shop and I eventually purchased the instrument. It had been owned by Bub Jones, Stan's brother, who used to play in swing bands in the 1940s and 1950s in Wagga. Unfortunately, it was not in very good shape – the sides had become partially detached from the back consequently, getting any sort of decent sound out of it was remote as the unjoined timber sides rattled against the back every time a string was played. It sat in a corner if my bedroom for years and eventually I moved it to my house in Wagga, suspended from the ceiling by a chain in my home office. In the early 1990s, after I had got into jazz, I decided to get serious about using the bass so I sent it to a luthier in Sydney to be done up, but it was beyond repair – he gave me $100 for the neck and said he would use the rest for firewood. I used the $100 towards a new double bass which he sent to me without any upfront payment – he said he could always trust a bass player!

Woody reckons we recorded ourselves on a little tape machine in my bedroom somewhere around 1968/69 but I think more likely 1966/67, me playing double bass and according to Woody, him playing a toothbrush holder [I suspect he was on guitar] – he sent me the tape for my 70th birthday [see **Odds and Sods and other stuff**].

Around this time, Woody and I both purchased new Vadis amps – according to Woody's diary, his was crap despite costing him £187! I vaguely remember mine but must have been happy enough with it because it lasted until destroyed in the 1968 disco fire [see **1968**]. These were the first amps any of the band owned with a separate head and speaker-cabinet as all our original amps were combos. The extra size of the amps added to the band look and the extra watts were always welcome. I always enjoyed feeling the bass pulses coming from the speaker box and hitting the back of my legs.

These days bands engage audio technicians with sophisticated digital gear to balance the sound from front of house – The Mystics sound, and what volume we each played at, was balanced by each of us individually on stage and I don't remember too many issues with one member being too loud. It did not take long for Les, Woody, Seymour and myself to establish what volume to use and mostly, irrespective of the venue, these same volume settings were used at just about every venue. I used to like The Rock Hall because, for some reason, it resonated with the bass particularly on a D note played on the A string, and gave it a fatter sound. Other halls and venues had the same affect and it was always the D note. Occassionaly the band might have been approached to "turn it down a bit", always by a person of advanced age!

Christmas Eve Dance

The band was booked for a dance at The Rock Hall on Christmas Eve – Porky, unbeknown to the rest of us, had the day off in Jerilderie so he had a few Christmas drinks with his Jerilderie mates before heading home later in the day. He stopped at Urana and/or Lockhart for a couple extra on the way home so understandably, by the time he turned up at the hall, he was shot – it was a long night for the rest of the band as Porky tried to keep up – never a good gig when the beat keeper is pissed and can't keep beat! This would not be the first and only time Porky turned up to a gig after a day on the grog but fortunately for the rest of the band, it did not become a habit.

New Year's Eve

The band was booked for a New Year's Eve dance at the Pleasant Hills Hall. According to Les, and confirmed by Porky, the crowd was massive – so much so that Les remembers that one third of the crowd was in the hall [packed to the rafters] and there were another two thirds outside. The size of the crowd was confirmed by the fact that the pub at Pleasant Hills was drunk dry and they had to send into Henty for more supplies. Both Les and Porky said that it was as "hot as shit" that night and the night was a great success. Julie McGrath can remember this night and confirms that it was a big crowd – she and her mum, her aunty and cousin all went out to Pleasant Hills for the night. Unfortunately, the only Henty Observer paper missing for 1966 was the very last edition which would have contained an ad for this dance. Most likely it was for the Pleasant Hills Rural Youth group, which held regular dances at the hall, but their dance ads never mentioned what band was playing.

Woody's Gig Diary

Woody had kept gig diaries and fortunately for this history, was able to locate them for 1966, 1967 and 1969. The Rock dances were never advertised in any local paper which suggests that Julie McGrath's posters, and word of mouth, were the only way the dances were advertised! Woody's diary for 1966 starts in June, so there is a period of about 3 months after Woody joined the band in February that gigs can't be identified. Unfortunately, Woody did not keep records of the venues played or what we earned – he simply put a line through the date in the diary of every gig we played. Despite the lack of detail, it shows that the band was working consistently in its first year and even though there is no evidence, every two weeks the band played a dance at The Rock!

Gigs for the year

The band had been getting reasonably consistent work for a new band with 4 gigs in April and June, 2 in July but then 6 in August with 5 in September, 2 in October and 5 more in November finishing off the year with 4 in December- the bulk would have been for the Swimming Pool Committee. The band did 34 identified gigs despite the gap between mid-February and June when Woody's diary started - not bad for a band in its first year and coming from a small town like The Rock.

1967

January started off quietly with only one identified gig in the month. However, January is remembered for the night I stacked Seymour's father's farm ute at the turn off into Kohlhagen's Beach at Collingullie. We had been to Kyeamba Smith Hall to see The Masters Apprentices in the supper room. Someone in the band had been told of a party at Lockhart, put on by some girls who were fans of our band, and we were all invited.

The night I crashed the Moore's farm ute!

I remember us drinking some large cans of beer outside the hall before we headed off to Lockhart during which it was suggested that we call in at Kohlhagen's Beach – a sandy bend in the Murrumbidgee River – for a swim in the dark on the way out. Seymour suggested I drive his ute as he had female company. Les was in his car and leading, and I was following Joe Brown, a mate of Porky's from Jerilderie, who was driving an FJ Holden. I had forgotten about the swim idea by the time we were approaching the turn off into the beach. Les slowed down to turn onto the dirt beach road which caused Joe to also reduce speed, and despite me standing on the brakes in a desperate attempt to slow down, we smashed into the rear of Joe's car.

The front panel of the ute had been pushed into the passenger side front tyre so the ute could not be driven. Les pulled a steel road sign out of the ground which pointed the direction to Kohlhagen's Beach, and which read "Impassable during wet periods", and tried to use it as a lever to get the panel off the tyre. Some passing vehicles pulled up to see if they could help, a carton of beer was produced, and the accident site turned into a party site on the side of the road. We eventually managed to free the tyre and headed back to The Rock. I was so worried about Jack Moore's reaction because of the damage to the front of his farm ute, I simply went home and went to bed but it didn't seem to worry Seymour - he was distracted for the night by his female interest, so he went over to Porky's place where they continued on with the party.

The next morning we reported the accident to the local copper, Craig Cunningham [who also played in the footy side], and he requested we take him out to the accident site – it was embarrassing as there were beer cans laying everywhere, an empty beer carton and a steel road sign left lying on the side of the road and which had obviously been vandalised. I was charged with negligent driving, and I appeared in court 6 months later. Surprisingly, Craig also attended court, gave the magistrate a nice character reference about me, and I was subsequently fined only $17 with $2 court costs and kept my licence.

Dance closed down

The Mystics first gig for the year was at The Rock Hall in late January but according to Woody's diary, it was shut down early because of a cyclone warning – a bit unusual for The Rock and rural Australia. I wonder if the punters got their money back and/or if we got paid?

Fund Raiser – Free Gig

In February 1967, the Tasmanian bushfires around Hobart caused significant loss and damage. I can't recall who organised it, but a fund-raising dance was held at The Rock Hall and the band agreed to do the gig as a freebie, which was a common thing as I found ads for other bands doing bushfire gigs at that time. I remember us feeling very pleased with ourselves for having been able to contribute.

The After 5 Club

The After 5 Club was at the back of the Golden Arcade [not there now] in the first block of Baylis Street, Wagga, and was started by Keith Bird in about January 1966. The place became a popular Sunday night dance venue and was Bevell's Restaurant when it wasn't being used for Sunday night dances and the resident band was Keith's band, The Cavaliers.

The venue had a non-alcoholic drinks bar and served small meals. The small stage, situated at the end of the dance floor, was low and had a drum riser – the crowd would be jammed right up against the band which added to the atmosphere! There was a small band room behind the stage. It was a great venue to play in because the sound was compacted by the small stage with the atmosphere of the crowd being jammed in, giving the place a great feel.

Nearly our first [and only] fight!

The band played for the first time at the After 5 Club for a private 21st birthday for Mick Walker on the 11th February with the party going from 8pm - 3.30am after which it continued at Mick's place, and the band was invited. We stayed for a while and as we were leaving to go home, Les was punched in the back of the head by a bloke he did not know – Les hit the bloke back and we bolted. In the rush to get to the cars, Porky jumped over something in the dark and into a rose bush. The bloke went back into the party and came back out with a couple of mates to carry on the punch-up. By this time, we were in the cars and as we were driving off, Woody was punched through the open car window and ended up with a black eye – Les says this was all over a one of the Pinnock girls, who was a top sort, but he can't recall who in the band might have been trying to crack on to her, if anyone! Despite the often attraction of girls to band players and the possibility/probability of a jealous boyfriend, The Mystics were only ever confronted with violence twice. The following weekend, the band played another 21st birthday for Dianne Spence, this time in the upstairs Pacific Lounge at the Wagga Leagues Club.

Les's Dying Amp

Les's Maton 4-speaker amp, which we all played through when we first started "rehearsals" in the church hall at The Rock, was starting to show signs of the overloads which it used to suffer. The speakers kept tearing and he had replaced a couple which was proving costly, so he decided to take a different approach. If a speaker started playing up, Les would get out his PMG pliers and simply cut the offending speaker out of the circuit. One night at Lockhart, Les cut out the third speaker which left him with only one of the four working, which caused the rest of us to wonder what happens when the remaining speaker starts to play up at a gig! I think the amp stayed that way until Les left the band.

The Shantines/The End and other Bands

The Shantines had been the top group in Wagga Wagga for a year or so and late in 1966 they changed their name to The End. The band was made up of Jacky McGrath, Terry Stirzaker, Mick Archer, Pat Geaghan and Geoff Maurer. In early 1967, the band decided to try its luck in the Melbourne music scene. Both Pat and Geoff decided to leave the band and Peter Nicol was recruited from Melbourne. Keith Bird says he got Peter through a connection with Eminar amps who ran a booking agency as well. The band continued as a 4-piece and spent a few months rehearsing in Wagga then in April 1967 they moved to Melbourne. Their departure for the big smoke opened up a couple of places for other bands – the After 5 Club and Kyeamba Smith Hall. An interesting side note – I found ads in the Tumut papers for a band called "The "Shaunteens" who did regular gigs in Tumut in 1966 – clearly the organisers had their own idea on the spelling of "Shantines"!

There were a few other bands who had been around for a few years and were getting plenty of gigs – The Corvettes, The Cavaliers, The RJs "featuring" Donny Crow, and The Blue Themes, all of whom were a bit tied to the late 50's, early 60's style of music. Lost and Found, who started about the same time The Mystics did, were regularly booked in venues in Wagga and seemed to have taken over from The Shantines/The End for gigs at Kyeamba Smith Hall and the After 5 Club. Keith Bird confirmed to me that, whilst he used them regularly, he really didn't take much to the style of music they played. They were a good R&B band and were playing different music to the mainstream bands. My research suggests that they did not do too many gigs in the smaller towns around Wagga as I only found a couple of ads for them in the regional papers I researched.

Tootool Woolshed Dance

The Mystics were booked whenever The Rock Yerong Creek Footy club held woolshed dances. One at the Vennel's woolshed at Tootool on the 6th May was a great night but it ended with Ronny Taylor writing off brother Colin Taylor's Vauxhall, after he had been sent into The Rock pub to get another keg. Trying to get back to Tootool as quickly as he could, Ronny took the bend at the War Memorial end of the Avenue in The Rock too fast causing the keg to move in the boot from one side to the other and as a result of the sudden weight transfer, he rolled the car up against the fence of the Seventh Day Adventist church. He wasn't injured but the car was a write-off and the beer never made it to the woolshed.

The band, from the beginning of the year, continued to be booked every two weeks for dances at The Rock by the Swimming Pool Committee and this continued throughout the year with the benefit being that the committee was making money from the dances and the band was getting plenty of gigs and practice at The Rock thus becoming more proficient and popular with the result that bookings were now coming in regularly from other towns.

The Mystics very first advertised gig in Wagga was a two-band gig

The Mystics had played at the After 5 Club earlier in the year for a private 21st party but this gig on the 7th May was the band's first official booking by a dance promoter in Wagga. It was a two-band gig with the Ever-Changing Minds from Albury. In terms of band history, none of the band has any recollection of this important Wagga gig! Another After 5 Club booking for the band a week later was cancelled, reason not recorded.

John Hetherington's 21st Birthday

John worked with Les and Porky at the PMG and I think he had attended Mick Walker's 21st at the After 5 Club earlier in the year. He obviously liked the band that night, so he booked The Mystics to do his 21st birthday night at the North Wagga Hall in May. I remember this night for two reasons. Firstly, a couple of kids who had been at boarding school, one from Tumut and the other from Sydney, turned up at the hall [I don't know how they found out I was playing in the band there] – I hadn't seen them for about 3 years. The other thing I remember is that John's mother was very sick with cancer at the time and she couldn't attend the party so she had a tape recording made of her speech to him, which was played to the whole crowd in the hall. There was hardly a dry eye in the place.

Henty Gigs

The band played for the "Grand Opening" of Henty's Mod dance on the 17th June at the Henty Memorial Hall with the ad for the gig describing the band as "Fabulous Mystics", which seems to indicate that the band's reputation preceded its first appearance in Henty. The band would play three gigs there over the next three months.

The "Fabulous" Mystics - the first band to play at the Mod dances in Henty!

I remember after one of these Henty gigs, the girls were hanging around the back of the hall whilst we were packing up and Porky offered to give them all a kiss if they lined up – which a lot did, and which he did!! Local twin sisters were two Henty fans who were very appreciative of the band's appearance in Henty and always turned up when we played in the town.

Grannies

The Mystics were booked to play in Wagga again, but this time at Grannies, and it may have been the first, or certainly one of the very early gigs, at this venue.

The "Mighty" Mystics!

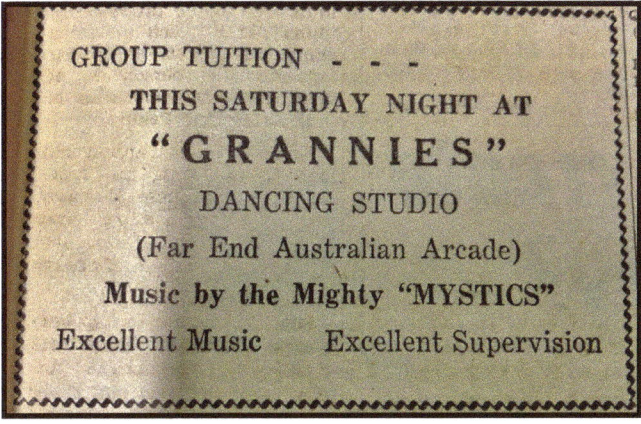

Grannies was a joint venture operated by Keith Bird and Peter Morrow, a Wagga businessman. Keith had been successfully running dances at Kyeamba Smith Hall and the After 5 Club and when he lost temporary access to Kyeamba Smith Hall as a venue for a few months, he decided to open another dance venue. Peter Morrow had an upstairs room above his shop in the Australian Arcade and this was converted into Grannies. The Mystics played this venue on the 24th June and I distinctly remember Les playing there with a missing front tooth and stitches in his lip, the result of a football injury received in the game against Collingullie that day. Grannies was a great place to play with a small stage at the back end of the room - it did not last long because of complaints about the noise from residents who lived on the floors above the venue. It appears that Grannies was subsequently moved to the Wollundry Room, under 2WG, the local Radio Station.

Les remembers the band's one and only gig at Boree Creek on the 1st September because the fog was so thick driving home after the gig, he was almost down to walking pace in the car, especially around the bends at Milbrulong. Dances in little town halls were always very well attended even if it involved a bit of travelling to get to them.

One of the great things of playing in a band was that, from the stage, we were able to see all the girls on the dance floor and despite our relative inexperience, it didn't take long to master the trick of picking out a good looking girl, continuing to follow her around the dance floor until she noticed that she was a point of interest even though she might have been dancing with her boyfriend. The trick was to then to look elsewhere and pretend to be interested in someone else but steal an occasional glance back, and invariably the girl would be looking at you – she would respond with a sly smile to signify your interest was reciprocated. A great way to increase the fan base but also a sure way to piss off the boyfriend if you were caught!

The band continued to work consistently, playing gigs at district halls, sometimes doing two gigs a weekend. In June, Woody has a note in his diary about The Battle of the Sounds – Seymour can remember us talking about it but can't remember if we took part in the contest – no-one else can recall anything about this although I expect we would have been keen to take part and test ourselves against the other bands, but it seems we passed on the opportunity.

On a date in early July, "Porky injured" is all that appears in Woody's diary – no mention of a gig that might have been cancelled or if Porky played despite the injury. The band appeared again at The After 5 Club on the 3rd September, this time playing the whole night without a support band. It was at this gig that the Wagga Daily Advertiser took a photo of the group in full flight and interviewed me about the band. An article and photo appeared in the DA on the 15th September under the heading "Football goes with Pop music". The article that accompanied the photo caused a bit of concern because both Porky and Les were listed as working for the PMG and at that time, government employees were not allowed to earn money from a second job, however, nothing eventuated. Up to this point in my research in the Wagga Daily Advertiser [January 1966 to September 1967], we were one of only two bands to be featured with a photo and article – the other was Wagga's top group The Shantines! This gig was Woody's last night before having to take leave from the band for 2 months to study for his HSC and the paper article announced that Pat "Gaghan" [sic] would replace Woody. It also alluded to the fact that the footy team hadn't been all that successful in 1967. The Mystics played a total of six gigs at the After 5 Club between May and November in 1967 making it one of the more regular and, by extension, more popular bands to play this venue considering the number of bands available in Wagga at the time.

Many of the bands that were operating in Wagga simply never got an opportunity because Keith Bird was pushing the newer bands rather than the bands that had been around for a few years – maybe the newer bands weren't that hungry for the money and were cheaper! This was an indication that The Mystics had started to establish itself in the Wagga music scene whilst at the same time, continuing

The paper article and photo from the band's third appearance at the After 5 Club

to play many gigs in the smaller towns around The Rock. Seymour remembers playing one gig at the After 5 with a front tooth missing following a football match on the Saturday – he reckons it's hard to sing whilst at the same time trying to keep the gap, left by the missing tooth, covered by his top lip.

Pat Geaghan Fills In

Woody, who was in his final year at school, had to pull out of the band as his mother did not want him being distracted in his HSC exam studies by band work consequently, the band needed a temporary guitarist. I knew Pat Geaghan because he was in The Shantines/The End and fortuitously, Pat had been in the class with me doing a repeat year at Wagga High in 1966, and we had become friends. Pat had withdrawn from The End earlier in the year when they decided to go to Melbourne and was doing fill-in gigs with other bands. Whilst I saw out the extra year of school in 1966, Pat had had enough and left school halfway through the year. I would often slag off school of an afternoon and head over to Pat's house on the side of Willan's Hill where we would discuss music and he would show me things to improve my playing.

I filled Pat in on the issue with Woody pulling out and he readily agreed to join The Mystics for the time that Woody would be missing but stipulated that it would only be for the period Woody was unavailable – he wasn't all that interested in a full-time commitment to playing in a band again. Pat had a Fender Stratocaster which he used through a Fender Twin Reverb amp. Pat began rehearsing with us almost immediately so that he was ready to take over when Woody left, and the first gig he did with the band was a Woolshed dance for The Rock Yerong Creek Footy Club at Edward's woolshed at Yerong Creek. Seymour remembers this gig because he said it was a great night and that we played well with Pat in the band for the first time.

As Woody was out of the band there was no need for him to record upcoming gig dates consequently only a few gigs have been identified in the two months that he was out of the band. One identified gig was another night at the After 5 Club where The Mystics played on the 1st October for a long weekend Midnight to Dawn gig. Again, no-one can remember this gig even though it was the first time the band had played until dawn!

Midnight to Dawn – a first for The Mystics

Whilst doing research for this history, the ads and paper items in the Youth Column showed that the band often played gigs on a Sunday night and is an indication of how vibrant the Wagga music scene was at this time, yet I only ever remember the After 5 as a Sunday gig – it was possible to play three gigs over a weekend and the band did this on a number of occasions [**see Gig Guide**].

With very few gigs being identified in the period that Woody was out of the band, as can be seen from the Gig Guide, and because the band had been working consistently, it is reasonable to assume that this continued during Woody's absence. One of these gigs would have been Pat's first Swimming Pool dance at The Rock, the first time the locals saw an outsider from The Rock or Yerong Creek, in the band. The 2WG Wollundry Room, which was situated downstairs and under the radio station was the band's next identified Wagga gig on the 5th November, another Sunday night gig which appears to be Les's last with The Mystics.

The Hardest Decision

Once Woody had finished his exams, he was ready to re-join the band but a problem had arisen. Pat, who had initially said that he only wanted to fill in for Woody for the 2 months, had enjoyed playing with The Mystics and being part of the band so much that he had changed his mind and wanted to continue with the band. Porky, Seymour, Woody and I decided that we didn't want a 6 piece band and that Les would have to unfortunately finish up as we felt that he had not progressed in his musical ability at the same pace the rest of us had. Additionally, Pat was now handling all the work on new songs and sang high harmony and with Woody back, the vocals would be so much stronger and better with three-part harmony when needed. I recall the four of us having a meeting out on the Mangoplah Road one afternoon about who would get the job of telling Les he would have to finish up with the band. The decision was decided by drawing matches and I ended up with the short one – delivering the bad news to Les was something I did not want to do but for the band to improve, needed to be done. Telling an original member and mate who had been the first to own a guitar, buy an amp, who had driven some of us to gigs and rehearsals and who we played footy with, that he was out of the band, was a very hard thing to do. I can't recall anything about my conversation with Les, but it would have been very difficult, for both of us! When the news broke, it split The Rock. It wasn't taken very well, which we expected, and the town was divided by Les's forced exit from the band. Pat copped a bit of criticism about breaking up the band and friendships, but unfortunately for Les, the decision stood. To his great credit, he did not hold any ill feeling towards any of us and he still followed the band and the blow may have been somewhat softened by the fact that he could spend more time with his girlfriend, Carol. A similar thing happened to Pete Best who was The Beatles original drummer – he got axed just as they were about to take off as it was considered that he was holding the band back and didn't fit the image they were after – the difference was that The Beatles never ever spoke with him again but we remained mates with Les!

Pat's Influence

As Pat was more experienced musically and was a bit of a master with chord variations, after joining on a temporary basis, he naturally assumed the job of working out chords for new songs and this now

continued with him as a full-time member of The Mystics. His experience and musical knowledge added more to the band, and we improved as a result. The band was doing a lot of British band's songs –The Beatles, The Hollies, The Kinks, The Animals, and various other bands. Around this time we did a song by the Bee Gee's, "Spicks and Specks", remembered solely because of an old piano on the stage at The Rock Hall, slightly out of tune, which Pat used for the first and only time we used a keyboard in the band at The Rock.

As I worked in Wagga, Pat would pick me up after work on rehearsal nights and we would buy fish and chips [wrapped in newspaper, the only way to eat them] and a large bottle of Coca Cola at a cafe in the top block [not there now] and then drive out to Moore's Woolshed.

Pat in his usual band gear

Pat had an FJ Holden with a column gear shift which often smelled like a fish and chip shop! As he was a non-drinker, it is possible that Pat's almost life-long consumption of Coca Cola, may have contributed to his diabetic issues later in life.

Greg Verdon's recollection is that the band really took off musically after Pat joined and he noticed a change in the type of music the band was playing. He remembers the band doing "You keep me hanging on", by Vanilla Fudge, a favourite of his as well as "The Shapes of things" by The Yardbirds – interesting, as I don't recall playing this song at all although I liked it! From the early days when we played mostly easy pop stuff, Pat's inclusion allowed us to become more adventurous with song selection and with Woody and Pat able to provide good harmonies, our song list took on a broader range of styles although we still kept to mainly pop songs which now often had psychedelic overtones, which we could never produce on stage but which didn't stop us adding these types of songs to the list.

The 2nd Jerilderie Gig

The second trip to Jerilderie, now with Pat in the band, was on the 18th November. For a bit of a stir, on the way out to Jerilderie, he decided to pretend he was a druggie just for a bit of fun with the locals so from the time we arrived, he pretended to be spaced out, vague and distant. He kept up this pretence for an hour or so, but nobody took any notice! After all, it was Jerilderie where just about anything went!

Again, the hall was packed, and it was a great night for the band. After the gig we went down to the local Billabong Creek to light a fire and have a few beers. Porky decided to drag a log up the bank of the creek, slipped and fell into the water. Showing no common sense at all, and probably affected by alcohol, fully clothed, I dived into the creek thinking that he had fallen into deep water – there was no real need for this show of heroics as the water turned out to be only about two feet deep which I discovered when I dived in! I think the band all slept at one of the pubs that night. Seymour covered himself in anything but glory because he woke up the next morning under the bed, with both his curly hair and the bed he'd been sleeping in for part of the night, covered in what he had eaten and drunk the night before!

The Final Four

On the 19th November, the band formerly from Wagga and known as The End, returned to the After 5 Club for their first gig in the city since leaving for Melbourne. They were now under their new name, The Final Four. I remember this night in some detail as they blew the crowd away, they had improved so much even though they were already very good when they left Wagga.

The Final Four

Woody and me at the After 5 Club to see The Final Four – Woody's occupied, I'm not!

I remember Mick Archer with almost Afro hair - we regarded him as a great drummer. Peter Nichol had his guitar "F" holes taped up I think to stop feedback – he always reminded me of Terry Britten from The Twilights. Jacky really looked the part of lead singer and played keyboards/ organ. I remember Terry [my former un-paid bass teacher] on stage with a pair of pants that had a little split in the front pleat which allowed the bottom of the pants to fall either side of his shoes. It looked very cool and his bass playing, which I was always a fan of, was even better. They had for a short while, after moving to Melbourne, been Ronnie Burns backing group. I can still recall the very first morning I heard their record "Grand Central Station" on 2WG – nice harmonies and a great little tune. I think Molly Meldrum originally thought they were an American group when he first heard their record and gave it a real wrap! They were a great small band renowned for their Beatles medley but unfortunately, they eventually had to change to a bigger sound and became The Dream with two extra members.

St Joseph's Hall

Situated on the corner of Tarcutta and Johnson Streets, Wagga, and part of St Joseph's Primary School, "St Joey's" was a regular dance venue. The Mystics first appeared here on the 25th November at a dance put on by the YCW. It was one of the early gigs the band played with Woody back in the band and Pat permanently replacing Les. St. Joeys became a regular gig for the band over the next couple of years.

Over the years, a regular venue for both The Mystics and Collection

Whilst the date cannot be identified, Porky recalls one of the gigs at this venue was poorly attended and only a few punters turned up. After an hour or so, the organiser approached Pat to advise that, as there seemed no likelihood of the usual crowd turning up, he would close the dance down early and consequently asked Pat what the cost would be for an early end to the night. According to Porky, Pat asked the organiser what he had been quoted and the bloke responded with the amount, expecting a discount but Pat spoiled his expectation by confirming that what he had been quoted would also be what he would be paying! Pat's reasoning – there was no way we would get another gig that night to make up for any shortfall in gig fee and it wasn't our problem that the crowd didn't turn up! Other dance venues in Wagga were the Purple Eye Disco Au Go Go [unable to find out where this was held] and The Teen and Twenty Club at St Johns Parish Hall. From memory, I don't recall The Mystics ever playing at St Johns but as has been mentioned earlier, Les believes the band played at St Johns in the very first few gigs the band did in 1966.

Ronnie Burns

"Go Set" was the magazine all bands read because it was all about bands, both Aussie and from overseas. Molly Meldrum was heavily involved with the publication and every year the magazine ran a popularity poll in respect to bands and singers. Ronnie Burns was voted Australia's Top Male Singer in a poll conducted by the magazine in 1967 and was brought to Wagga by After 5 Promotions to appear at the Kyeamba Smith Hall and The Mystics were booked as his backing band. The date was the 2nd December, and this would be the band's first major gig. I remember setting up the gear early on the Saturday afternoon at Kyeamba Smith Hall and Ronnie and

Our biggest gig since forming the band – backing Ronnie Burns at Kyeamba Smith Hall and playing to 1500 kids!
L to R: Brownie, Woody, Ronnie, Pat obscured by Jeff Joseph, Ronnie's manager

his manager, Jeff Joseph, came in. Ronnie was a nice bloke and we got on well with him. I can only recall one number he did, "Coalman", which was his last record - he would have also done probably 5 or 6 other songs. I don't remember any charts being produced [not really a thing in those days]. We would have had a couple of run-throughs and most likely he simply did numbers that we were already doing – we had Bee Gee's numbers on our song list which he probably would have done as they wrote Coalman and sang back-up on the record. I remember that we got changed into our gig gear at Marty Ward's mother's place in Ashmont – I wore striped pants I had made by Winter, the lady Pat worked with at a curtain shop in the Australian Arcade – the pants were made out of curtain material and Pat had had a pair made as well.

About 1,500 kids turned up that night to hear Ronnie, and by association, us! After the gig ended, we were invited back to The Astor Motel where Ronnie was staying with his manager indicating that he appreciated our backing. After talking with him for an hour or so, we left in the early hours of the morning to find that Woody's car was filled with what appeared to be white smoke and as soon as he opened the door to see what the problem was, the interior of the car burst into flames. Someone rushed off to call the fire brigade but Ronnie had seen what was happening and quickly came down the stairs from his room with a plastic bucket and proceeded to put the fire out using water from the swimming pool that used to be at the back of The Astor. By the time the fire brigade arrived, it was all over bar the smell of burnt car interior – the car belonged to Woody's parents. I remember Kevin Verdon, who was in the police force in Sydney, telling Porky that he had heard a radio interview with Ronnie on a station in

Sydney and Ronnie had told the story of the fire in the car in Wagga – it must have been not long after. Many years later, I was talking with him at a corporate conference in Tasmania and I asked him if he remembered but he could not recall the event at all – what a bummer!

The reason for the fire was that it appeared that, whilst we were packing up at the end of the night, someone had flicked or dropped a cigarette butt into the large cardboard box that Woody kept the amp speaker in when not in use. He then loaded it onto the back seat of his parent's car and drove the car to The Astor. By the time we came to leave, the cardboard box had been smouldering and using up oxygen for some time as the car was locked. The second Woody opened the car and let fresh oxygen in, the cardboard box and seat burst into flames. Woody's speaker box and the back seat were severely damaged – he thinks he bought a replacement box even though he didn't like the amp. This would not be the band's only loss by fire!

Christmas Eve Dance

Again, the band was booked for this dance at The Rock and again Porky got stuck into the grog during the day at Jerilderie before heading home. I remember getting word that Porky had arrived home but was at The Rock pub, so I had to go over and get him to come and play the gig. He was flyblown! During one song he managed to fall off the drum stool mid-song and whilst it was funny to a lot of the crowd, I remember getting stuck into him about things being professional in the little back room we used during set-breaks – Seymour also had a crack at him and Porky, probably feeling the heat, responded by saying "OK, Mario Lanza!" [Mario Lanza was a popular American Italian opera singer from some years before] - Seymour has never forgotten the comparison and whilst it was serious at the time, now it's one of those funny incidents! Thankfully, Porky never turned up drunk again to play!

When we played at The Rock, I used the family car to get my gear to the hall, and when the gig was finished, pack the gear into the car and head home, leaving the gear in the car to be unpacked the next day. On Christmas Day, after the dance the night before, I went out to unload my gear and noticed that my bass case, which had been laying on the back seat with the car unlocked, was not as heavy as it usually was. On opening it up to see why, I was horrified to see my bass missing, and in its place a small toy guitar. I was shattered – my beautiful bass was gone! I raced inside to tell my mother that my bass had been stolen and she burst out laughing – she had removed my bass from its guitar case before I woke up, and replaced it with the toy guitar as a Christmas Day joke – despite the relief, I could have killed her and I didn't see the funny side of the joke, at all! What non-musicians don't appreciate is that musicians get very attached to their instrument[s].

WAGGA FAREWELLS 1967 Festival

About 1000 teenagers attended a "Monster Dance," staged by the Fund at Kyeamba Smith Hall, to hear The Mystics, The Climax Five and pop star, Bobby Thomas.

New Year's Eve

The band was booked for a dance at Kyeamba Smith Hall on New Year's Eve by the Wagga Community Advancement Fund. It was a two-band gig with The Climax 5, who had a record out in 1968 called "Gardens" which bombed. As well, Bobby Thomas was on the bill and I don't think we knew too much about him either – he had a bit of a career more so into the 1970's. Whilst I can very vaguely remember being on stage that night, none of the band recalls the night at all consequently it cannot be established if we, or The Climax 5, backed Bobby. As can be seen from the above section out of the front-page news item, it was reported that 1000 kids were at the dance. The band's appearances at Kyeamba Smith Hall to this point had been limited to two gigs in December and it wasn't until late 1968 and 1969 when the band was to appear at this venue on a regular basis.

Woody's Gig Diary

Woody's gig diary for 1967 contained a lot of information. We regularly earned £25 per gig which meant £5 each. Woody obviously had trouble with decimal currency because he had gig payments in the old currency, pounds [£], but dollars had been the currency for nearly two years. Notwithstanding, £25 a night was a very good earner compared to what we all would have been earning from our day jobs. The Jerilderie gig paid $100 – "fantastic" according to Woody's diary! I can't remember whether those driving their cars to the gigs got extra petrol money, but I expect they did. The diary also showed that we continued to work on a regular basis at The Rock Hall and Lockhart, both at the Memorial Hall Supper Room and the Golf Club. It also revealed that we did two gigs at Walla Walla, my old boarding school town and organised by an old boarding school girlfriend and her sister, plus gigs at Culcairn, Jerilderie, Boree Creek, Lake Albert Hall and Collingullie. This information from Woody covered large parts of the band's gigs which would most likely not be available from any other source. The band did 60 identified gigs during the year notwithstanding Woody being out of the band for two months and therefore no diary of gigs for that period! Despite only a couple of identified gigs, The Mystics would have worked consistently during Woody's absence.

Gigs for the Year

The band played at The Rock Hall often and the fans always supported the band, particularly in the early years, 1966 and 1967 – whilst gigs at The Rock Hall could not be specifically identified from Woodie's diary for 1966, the band played 16 times at the local hall in 1967 which suggests that most likely the band played a similar number of gigs in 1966 because the Swimming Pool Committee had hit on a very good fund raising earner – book The Mystics and run a dance. In 1967 the band also played 12 gigs in Wagga, 8 gigs at Lockhart and 7 gigs in Henty showing that it had established fan bases outside The Rock and in relation to Henty and Lockhart, way ahead of any other band in terms of appearances in the towns.

During the year, the band played consistently with 9 gigs in both May and November, 8 in June and 7 in December being the heaviest months. A limited number of gigs have been recorded in September and October which would not reflect the true gig numbers except for the usual fortnightly gig at The Rock Hall – other gigs could not be identified and Woody wasn't keeping a diary when he was temporarily out of the band.

1968

The Mystics playing to a huge crowd at the Wagga Memorial Gardens for the crowning of Miss Wagga 1968 - and for a change, Porky is in shot!

The year kicked off with a big gig on the first day of the new year at a Mardi Gras put on by the Wagga City Council. The band played on an outdoor stage to a huge crowd estimated by the local paper at about 8,000 that night in the Memorial Gardens for the presentation of the Miss Wagga Entrants and the ultimate crowning of Miss Wagga. Woody's gig diary notes that for this gig, Seymour's voice was stuffed from the New Year's Eve dance at Kyeamba Smith Hall the night before. Interestingly, The Mystics had played to crowds of 1500, 1000 and 8000 in a month.

With Pat now permanently in the band, it was decided that as he was in Wagga and we were getting more gigs at venues in Wagga, he should permanently run our bookings. He also continued in the role of working out new songs for practice every week. At the time I don't think the rest of the band really appreciated the amount of work involved working out the chords and writing down the words to new songs as Pat often bought two or three new songs to rehearsals. It was also notable that all the items about the band in the Daily Advertiser Youth Beat Column were as a result of Pat staying in contact with the journalist, which in turn contributed to the band being regularly mentioned in the column and which had an influence on the band's popularity.

We rehearsed at The Rock Hall on a Saturday afternoon when we were playing there that night, but practices were generally held on a Sunday afternoon at Moore's woolshed before Porky headed back to Jerilderie. Rehearsals were sometimes held with a shed full of sheep and occasionally, some of the local fans would turn up to listen whilst we rehearsed.

A break in practice at Moore's woolshed with a couple of fans - this was after Pat joined the band – his blue Fender is in the bottom left corner – must have been a hot day – seems like singlets were still in vogue and long socks with shorts were the fashion!

The Mystery Solved

The following photo was a complete mystery until I spoke with Jock McKenzie after more than 50 years [more about Jock later in this story]. Jock remembered this night very well, even down to the colour of the shirt he was wearing. It was a two-band gig at Kyeamba Smith Hall although I was not able to find a paper ad for it! It would have been in either late December 1967 or early January 1968. The photo is of The Mystics and The Generation of Love, Des and Jock's band. Jock says we were stuffing around – the two interesting things are that Porky, who was left-handed and didn't know a single chord formation, was on Woody's right-handed guitar, and Woody, who I doubt had any drumming experience, was on drums. To add to the confusion, Seymour is nowhere to be seen. I originally thought it was the night that we backed Ronnie Burns but the ad for that night does not mention Jock's band consequently, it seems like it was just another night at the showgrounds. Some of the punters around the front of the stage seem interested, whilst others seem totally uninterested as to what is going on up on stage! As the interested fans are up close, things must have sounded OK!

The Mystics and The Generation of Love, on stage at Kyeamba Smith Hall
L to R: Brownie, Porky, Jock McKenzie, Des Condon [obscured], Noel Hargreaves, Woody [at the back] and Pat

Subway

Subway was a new discotheque opened on the 20th January by local businessmen who decided to become dance promoters and The Mystics were asked to be the resident band. The venue was set up to cash in on the music scene in Wagga at the time and to compete with Keith Bird's promotions at Kyeamba Smith Hall, which were very successful. Subway was situated in the top block of Baylis Street on the station side of the Victoria Hotel. It had previously been Huthwaite's Manchester store which had been closed. The venue was to operate generally on a Friday and/or Saturday night and The Mystics, as resident band, were to play both nights, sometimes with a visiting band or singer from the big smoke, excluding the nights The Mystics had bookings elsewhere – on these nights, the promoters would get in other bands to fill the night. The bands or singers came from Melbourne, Sydney and Brisbane but as Keith Bird had been operating successfully bringing acts to Wagga for some time, he had tied up most of the top line acts, consequently, Subway was only able to bring in second-tier acts which were still reasonably well-known and popular. The Mystics used the venue for rehearsals usually on a Saturday afternoon, and after the gigs we stored our gear in a locked windowless storeroom on the premises to which Pat had the only key.

The opening night of Subway and an indefinite residency for The Mystics

Izzy Di and Adrienne

The Mystics played the opening Saturday night and the next night, Sunday, the band backed Izzy Di and Adrienne. I could only find "Issy De" on the net but no mention of Izzy Di or Adrienne. No-one remembers rehearsing with them but clearly, we would have. I don't think they had any songs out at the time – Issy De had more success in the 1970's. Verdo remembers them appearing at Subway and that Adrienne was a good-looking sort! He said he was talking with her out in the little

Izzy Di and Adrienne with Pat and Porky – clearly enjoying themselves and our backing

The Mystics in full flight at Subway!

courtyard behind the stage either during a break or at the end of the night and he thinks they/we did Vanilla Fudge's version of "You keep me hanging on", and during discussion he got a very negative reaction from Adrienne when he said he preferred The Supreme's version. When the band backed singers, I think the singers basically did songs we normally did and maybe one or two others. The issue after all this time is about what rehearsal was done with these acts. The band clearly would have had to do some rehearsal – backing acts would have been a disaster without some idea of songs and arrangements yet not one band member can remember rehearsing with any of the singers the band backed. It must have been a bit daunting for these acts to come out into the regional areas and to be backed by local bands because they would just have to accept the backing standard, good, bad or indifferent - promoters simply relied on local bands. My memory is that The Mystics provided good backing and I don't recall any problems or complaints.

Somebody's Image

The following week it was Somebody's Image with lead singer Russell Morris, who not long after was to become a huge solo artist. During one of their sets, Morris got upset with his band for some reason, or because he felt we were sounding better, and walked off the stage and left the band to complete their set without him. I have a vague recollection of talking with one of the blokes from Somebody's Image between sets out in the little courtyard behind the stage and he said that it was not unusual for Morris to "chuck a willy".

The night Russell Morris spat the dummy

The Boat Trip to NZ

Before the band got the residency at Subway, Seymour and I had booked a holiday to New Zealand for a couple of weeks in February. We sailed from Sydney to Auckland on a Greek ship called the Ellinis and the trip lasted 3 days and nights. On one of the nights there was a passenger talent quest in the main auditorium. Seymour entered and I accompanied him on acoustic guitar – I think it must have belonged to one of the other passengers we met on the boat. Seymour sang "Congratulations" by Cliff Richard and I remember rehearsing with the ship's Greek band in the afternoon and found that, even though none spoke any English, yelling out C D G and the rest of the chords, they understood. The band did a great job, the song went over well, the ship didn't sink and Seymour and I virtually had no sleep at all over the three nights on board – we were absolutely stuffed from partying by the time we got to Auckland.

Whilst we were there, we went out to a dance in Hamilton and saw this great little band, who were local kids just like us! I think they may have played "Tin Soldier" by The Small Faces which had been released in December and was high on the charts – an absolute ball-tearer of a song! We went out and bought the record and flogged it on the record player at the flat where we were staying and this was the first song where I was able to pick out the chord progression by simply listening to the song – clearly music was making more sense to me by this stage and Pat's influence was rubbing off.

The Mystics – 3-piece with Pat on my bass and Porky in the front line!

While Seymour and I were away, Lyn Randell and Klass, Ram Jam Big Band and The Cherokees [all from The Big Smoke] played in our place at Subway over 3 weekends. On the night The Cherokees were the guest band, Pat, Woody and Porky played a 3-piece set. This was hotly denied for years by Pat on the basis that whilst he and Woody might have sung a number or two normally in the band, they certainly would not have been able to carry a full set. Pat's denial was shot to pieces when I found photos of The Mystics 3-piece, in Pat's photo album, which indicates how long it had been since Pat looked at his photo albums – the photo shows additional amps on stage from our amps. Pat and Woody swapped between guitar and bass for the set. Porky has pinpointed the night because he recalls The Cherokees drummer using Porky's drum kit but his own snare. It seems the trio only played this one night. Following our return from NZ and after three weekends of guest bands, the paper ad for Subway announced, "Return of The Mighty Mystics"!

Marty Rhone

Marty Rhone, who was promoted as Australia's answer to Cliff Richard, was the next guest singer to appear. He had had a couple of singles released but they went nowhere however he did have a couple of bigger hits in the 1970's. He had a good voice with a high range so at rehearsals in the afternoon we asked him if he would do Tin Soldier, and he agreed – we were wrapt and that night, he/we did a great version but whatever else he did is anyone's guess! Whilst there is no memory of this as a regular thing, the photo shows Pat played keyboards/organ, which I think he owned and used when he was in The End – I can't remember it being brought to any other gigs at all - Pat was self-taught on keyboards and could play chords but had no bass left hand.

Marty Rhone with Pat on organ - probably doing Tin Soldier!

Around this time, a band from Leeton called The Syndicate was playing at the After 5 Club and when they finished for the night, they wandered over to Subway to listen to our band and they were impressed with the harmonies, to which I contributed nothing - one of the band members was Col Moses [see 1968] who comes into the story towards the end of the year.

From the beginning of March, The Mystics played two gigs each weekend for the first three weeks– at Tumut, St, Joseph's, Book Book and Coolamon [Friday and Saturday] with only three gigs at Subway – one at the beginning and two towards the end of the month, one being after the name change to Noah's. I didn't bother to research who was playing in our residency when we were gigging elsewhere!

Seymour's chauffeur

Verdo, despite being under-age for a driver's licence at the time, was often Seymour's chauffeur after dances, no matter where they were held. Verdo says Seymour was often half cut or tired or both after a gig [hard farm work and late nights at weekends the most likely reason] so Seymour would hand the keys to Verdo for the trip home. I assume that this was after Seymour had brought his own new Holden. Because of his age at the time, Verdo's mum only let him go to dances provided it was with Seymour - "Blue" McGrath often went along as well and Verdo reckons that it was The Mystics who put The Rock Hall on the map!

First Tumut Gig

In my day job, on a couple of occasions I had gone to Tumut with our company rep and one of the company's agents there had two daughters, who were very attractive and whom I had met a couple of times. I think it was through them that we were booked to play at the Church of England Hall by the Young Anglican Fellowship, which included an offer to stay overnight at the girl's place – their parents were there as well. I vaguely remember being in their house and that I was very interested in the older one and I think her sister was keen on Pat, but the connections went nowhere. I met the one I was keen on many years later and she had completely changed from a very stylish good-looker into a hairy arm-pitted "earth person" with matted hair who lived out in the hills somewhere around Tumut.

The Book Book Hall

The Mystics did two gigs at the Book Book Hall for the Book Book Tennis Club, the first one being in the heat of the late summer of 1968. This was an invitation only ball and is remembered by Seymour as the one and only time that he can recall "Blue" McGrath acting as a roadie for the band as well as collecting the money at the end of the night. It was also memorable for other reasons. Firstly, according to Seymour, "Blue" was dancing with a busty lady during the night and managed to slip and fall on top of her during the song, "When I'm Sixty-four". Secondly, according to Woody, the venue is also the site of a long remembered balancing act by Porky, performed on the yard structures adjacent to the hall. Thirdly, because one of the punters, a work colleague of mine, managed to fall over during one of our sets and broke his arm and spent most of the night at the Outpatients section of the Wagga Base Hospital.

Coolamon B&S

The Mystics were booked for a two night gig at Coolamon – on the Friday, a B&S Ball was held at the Golf Club, again by invitation only, and a Recovery night on the Saturday, which was held at a private rural property just on the outskirts of the town. The band must have played well at these two gigs because during Saturday night I recall being approached with an offer to play in Newcastle. Whether the offer was from a dance promoter wanting the band to play a number of gigs or simply a specific gig, the reason is lost to time.

Jon Blanchfield

The Subway promoters brought Jon Blanchfield from Brisbane for gigs over two nights in Temora and Wagga – he had had a bit of a hit with "Lavender Girl" and had only just started to hit the music scene.

Jon Blanchfield – a top bloke

Again, I am not sure when we got to rehearse with him because we played and backed him at Temora on Friday night and Friday was a workday for all of us. Anyway, we went over to Temora as a package deal on the 29th March. I do have a faint recollection of being in the Temora Hall, the only time we played in the town. Again, there is no memory of songs and it is most likely that Jon alternated the vocals with Seymour who shared some of our normal numbers with him. It was a two-band gig with a local group, The Wimowehs. The ad in the Temora Tribune says The Mystics were Wagga's "leading" group"! It appears this might have been the first time that a recording pop singer appeared in Temora. Woody actually recalls this night [one of the few] and reckons that the fans crowded around the back door when the night was over as we were packing up the gear – we were held up from leaving by dozens of girls waiting at the back of the hall and we had some trouble getting away – even Porky passed on the opportunity to emulate his effort with the girls at the Henty Hall.

After only 2 months, the promoters of Subway decided to change the name of the venue because they were losing out to Keith Bird. We were never told why but Jock's belief was that it was because it wasn't making enough money despite the crowds being good. This stands to reason as they had been paying us,

The Mystics getting ready to set up for another gig!

plus a singer and/or another band brought in from the big smoke, and the venue was competing against Keith Bird's dances at Kyeamba Smith Hall where hundreds of kids went.

Subway is now Noah's

Subway was closed for a week at the end of March whilst some renovations and changes were made included lining the venue with hessian, which apart from being a great sound deadener, was also a wonderful fire accelerant. The venue changed its name to "Noah's" and the first gig was held on the 30th March and from memory, a good crowd turned up to see "A great line-up of Stars"!

Subway re-opens as Noahs

Following the Friday night gig at Temora, Jon was also to appear at Noah's with the Laurie Allen Revue on the Saturday night, again with The Mystics providing his backing. Prior to heading to Noahs, we went to pick him up the from the Johnny Mac Hotel where he was staying. Porky spotted a red checked coat that Jon had hanging up and asked if he could wear it for the night, and Jon agreed. I think he might have had to wrestle Porky at the end of the night to get his coat back! I'm not sure if we did the song at Temora but we asked Jon about doing Tin Soldier at Noah's – he wasn't keen because it was not really in his voice range. Nonetheless, once he was on stage, we simply roared into the number and he had no option. He managed to get through the song, but it was a strain – it's been a source of a band joke ever since. Jon was a great bloke and we got on well with him despite the band putting him under enormous pressure.

The Laurie Allen Revue

On the same night, The Mystics played support for The Laurie Allen Review as well – their band included Wayne Duncan on bass and Garry Young on drums, both of whom went on to be part of the very successful Daddy Cool. The band also included Colleen Hewitt, who was one of the backing singers, [aged 16] and who went on to be crowned Queen of Pop – twice! At the end of the night we were invited to go back to the Johnny Mac Hotel, where they were all staying together with The Twilights, who had appeared at Kyeamba Smith Hall that night for After 5 Promotions. This was a real buzz for us because we liked The Twilights as a band and had a couple of their songs in our set list – "Cathy come home", "Young Girl" and "9.50".

The band continued to use Noahs as a rehearsal place and also to leave our gear on the premises and despite warnings from the promoters that there had been "attempted break-ins and we should take our gear home", we felt secure that the gear was safe in the storeroom because the only access was via the one door to which Pat had the only key.

Band Change - Garry "Jock" McKenzie

Around the time that the change of name to Noahs was happening, it seems that Seymour must have decided to leave the band, most likely because of the farm work and the pressure his father, Jack, was

putting on him about taking off early to get to gigs when there was work on the farm still to be done. Consequently, the search was on for another singer who suited the music we played. Des Condon had formed a new band, The Generation of Love, with Jock McKenzie on bass after Des left the Lost and Found at the end of 1966. Jock says that the band went for about 15 months and played gigs at Tumbarumba, Tumut, Urana and Jerilderie as well as at various Wagga venues but had broken up in early 1968 after which Jock headed off to Sydney for a short stint then returned to Wagga.

Jock remembers auditioning at Noahs one Saturday afternoon, along with two others, one of whom was a girl, for Seymour's vacancy in The Mystics. He says he got the call that night to say he was in the band – he reckons that the reason he got the job was that the girl wasn't a good looker! I doubt the band would have changed to a female singer irrespective of how good she was. Nothing is remembered about the third singer who auditioned! As we would be rehearsing at Noahs, Jock brought his PA system and bass amp and put them in the storeroom with the rest of our gear.

Garry "Jock" McKenzie – one of a kind

We rehearsed with Jock over the next two weeks as the band appears to have not had any gigs leading up to Easter Saturday night. Unfortunately for Jock, he never got to use his gear with The Mystics at a Noahs gig or even anywhere else!

Noah's Fire

On the night of the 13/14th April [Easter Saturday], Noahs suffered a severe fire, was completely gutted and all our stored gear including Jock's, was destroyed. Pat rang me early on the Sunday morning to tell me the news. Woody and I lost our amps and as well, Woody also lost his Elite guitar, Porky lost his drum kit and Jock lost his PA system, speakers, mikes, stands and his bass amp but Pat had taken both his Fender amp and Stratocaster home because he needed to work out new numbers for the band. Fortunately, Woody and I had insured our gear but Porky's set of drums, and Jock's gear, weren't covered.

Woody had left his guitar in the storeroom after we finished rehearsals, something he would not normally have done [both of us always took our guitars home but left our amps in the storeroom]. He was heading to Sydney and did not want to have his guitar in the car whilst he was floating around the city. He said that he was on his way back on the Sunday when he heard about the fire. It was unusual that the band had two weekends off between backing Jon Blanchfeld and when Noahs burnt down but maybe the two weeks was left free to allow Jock to get in some rehearsals with the band. Subway/Noahs had only been going for just under three months when it burnt down, and we were very suspicious of the origins of the fire because of the warnings we had been given about alleged break-ins and suggestions that we take our gear home.

Jock also confirmed that he had been approached by the operators with the attempted burglary story re his stored gear even though he had only just joined the band – this was suspicious! We went to the police about our concerns, but nothing ever happened. The hessian used as noise suppression under the ceiling and on the walls as a result of the reno completed a couple of weeks before, did a nice job of ensuring that everything went up! I don't think any of the owners contacted us about our loss of gear, and Noahs was no more! Whilst it hadn't been a financial success for the owners, it certainly gave The Mystics a higher profile in the Wagga music scene because it was the only dance venue in Wagga with a resident band and it gave the band experience [we played 8 gigs there in a couple of months] playing with some of Australia's well known professional bands and backing professional singers from the big smoke.

Keith Bird's Memories

I spoke with Keith Bird who has lived in Cairns for many years running a jewellery shop, to get his memories of this time in Wagga. Keith had been singing and playing rhythm guitar in The Cavaliers in the early 1960s, whilst at the same time, organising dances when the band had a night off. After a disagreement with their lead player, he left and became a very successful dance and band promoter, initially with the After 5 Club and then subsequently, with Kyeamba Smith Hall dances at the Wagga Wagga showgrounds. He also managed The Shantines/The End and would book top line groups or singers - Normie Rowe, John Farnham, Ronnie Burns, Johnny Young, The Twilights, The Masters Apprentices and The Groop were among many acts he brought to Wagga and often took them over to Griffith as well.

When Kyeamba Smith Hall became unavailable to him for a short time, he had a brief association with Peter Morrow, as already mentioned, with Grannies, at the back of the Australian Arcade above Morrow's shop. When Kyeamba Smith Hall became available again, Keith recommenced his bigger promotions. Morrow wanted to join Keith in the promotion's business, but Keith says he did not need a partner so Morrow and two or three other Wagga businessmen decided to set up a regular venue in opposition known as Subway, and it was to feature groups and pop singers from the big smoke. Because Pat worked for Morrow's business in the Australian Arcade, The Mystics were offered the job of resident band. Unfortunately for this venture, Keith Bird had the top acts tied up so that whenever Subway promoted a group or singer, Keith would bring in bigger acts and take out bigger ads for Kyeamba Smith Hall dances. An example was the Laurie Allen Revue, who were a new band on the music scene, at Noahs and The Twilights, who were at the time Australia's top band, at the showgrounds, on the same night.

A couple of times Keith Bird was approached by the people behind Subway to either join forces in dance promotion or run alternative nights rather than operating on the same nights in opposition to each other. Keith was confident that he had the better promotions venue and acts so was not interested in changing or merging his business. On the same weekend as the Noah's fire, Keith Bird had, as a special promotion, booked The Shadows to play in Wagga on Easter Monday at the old Plaza Theatre. After picking up Hank Marvin at Shepparton, where The Shadows played on Easter Saturday night, he drove back to Wagga on Easter Sunday and said he was "quite amused" when he turned into Baylis Street to see that Noah's had burnt down the night before.

Only a select couple of groups in Wagga continually benefited from his promotions. The Mystics and Collection did quite a few gigs at Kyeamba Smith Hall, the After 5 Club and Griffith for him and in fact, after The End and Lost and Found from 1966 to 1968, The Mystics and subsequently, Collection, were the most booked band by him between late 1968 to the end of 1969. When Keith finally pulled the pin on his promotions business, apart from Jimmy Logan's Wombat dances which started in 1968 and carried on into 1970, no other band and dance promoter had any success in the Wagga music scene.

The Fire – front page news! Pat and Jock with the burnt remains of some of our gear

The Shadows

Easter Monday night, 15th April, our early heroes, The Shadows, were appearing at the Plaza Theatre and as they were a strong early influence on all the band, we had booked seats for their show. I remember at the show, Mick Radatti, the guitarist for our arch-rivals, Captain Walker's Soul ["The Wall of Death" to us and formerly Lost and Found], offered to lend us their gear whenever they weren't playing, which was very generous of them, but we never did take up his offer. The other thing I remember about the night was that we were "disappointed" with The Shadows because they sounded exactly like their records - they were so good! I recently learned that a good friend of mine, together with a mate of his, actually moved The Shadows gear from Shepparton to Wagga and then took their gear on to Young after the Wagga gig yet he had no interest in music at all and just did it to help out!

New Gear

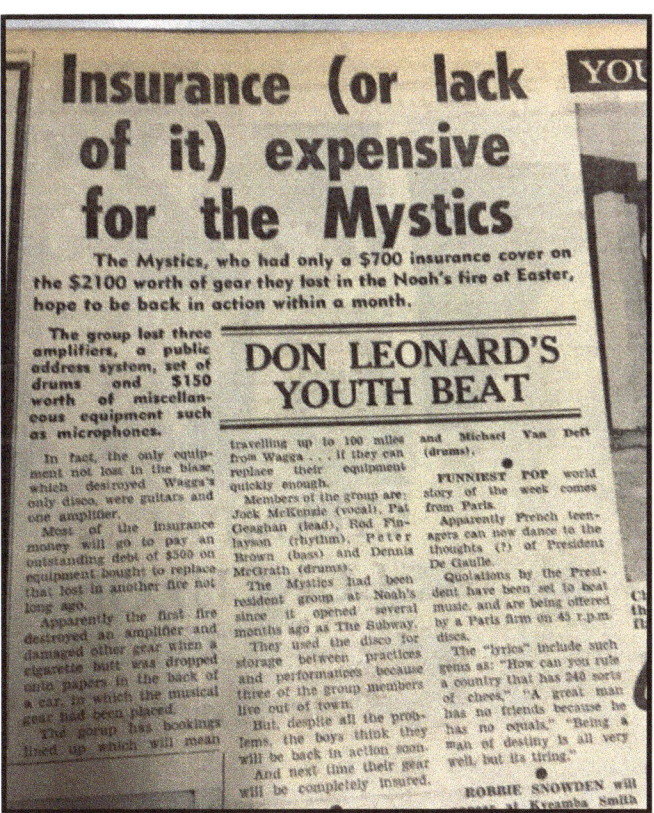

Following the fire at Noahs, we needed to get replacement gear and I found out that a distant relative was manufacturing Eminar amplifiers in Melbourne. Over the phone we ordered amps for Woody and me and new PA speakers and head for Jock - these were duly delivered to Pat a couple of weeks later and my father, Austen, handed over a cheque on behalf of everyone. Jock reckons that most of the band played the next 4-5 months for nothing as all the money had to go to paying off the debt.

Another headline!

According to Jock, we started practicing in a vacant shop next door to Stan Jones Harmony House which makes some sense as we had no rehearsal place in Wagga after the fire. He believed Stan Jones owned the building, but the arrangement came to a sudden stop when Stan found out we had purchased new gear directly from Melbourne rather than through him. Pat was not sure about this venue and could not remember any rehearsals there, nor could anyone else, but we obviously practiced somewhere and in the absence of any suggestions as to where that might have been, Jock's version seems credible.

> **MYSTICS GUITARIST,** Pat Geaghan is beginning to wonder if he is a "curse" on the group.
>
> Since he joined it in September last year the Mystics have encountered a seemingly unending run of problems.
>
> The drummer's car blew up on the way to a dance; a fire in the back of another car destroyed several hundred dollars worth of gear; at Easter the Noah's Disco fire destroyed Mystics' equipment valued at $2000; there has been a hold-up with getting replacement equipment; the fire also cut out regular Wagga work for the group.
>
> Now drummer Dennis McGrath has left the group, and guitarist Rod Finlayson has a broken finger, which will be in plaster for six weeks.
>
> And even then the continued use of his finger could be in doubt. This could mean an end to guitar playing for Rod.
>
> Despite these setbacks the group is quite confident of continuing — one way or another," one of the members told me yesterday.
>
> The Mystics will be playing at St. Joseph's Church Hall, Wagga, tomorrow night, and at The Rock on Saturday.

The paper highlighted the no-insurance problem experienced by some members of the band in an article in the Youth Beat column – Porky is still listed as being in the band so this was most likely during the period the band was out of action following the fire. I think Porky fully intended to continue, however, he eventually decided that he simply could not afford to buy a replacement kit and was consequently forced to pull out of the band. The band's connection to The Rock had now been reduced to me only.

Another snippet appeared in the paper relating to Pat and the bad luck he had brought with him, when he joined the band.

Pat's bad luck stories and it's confirmed – Porky leaves the band!

Band Changes

The first gig after our new gear arrived was played at The Rock Hall on the 11th May – slightly less than a month after the fire. This would have been an interesting night for Jock, fronting a band that came from the town which was used to seeing Seymour out front. According to the paper on the 6th June, Porky had left the group.

Robert "Dick" Kitney

Probably encouraged by Jock, we had offered the drumming job to Robert "Dick" Kitney. Dick had been playing in The Generation of Love with Jock in 1967 and was a pretty good drummer, however, Dick's move to The Mystics appears not to have made the Youth Beat column.

In May and June, the band played gigs at Yerong Creek, St. Joseph's and The Rock again with our only identified appearance in Henty for the whole year, on the 14th June. Jock's previous band, The Generation of Love scored one gig there earlier in the year. In the same article on the 6th June, among other problems the band had endured, it was reported that Woody had a "broken finger which might mean the end of his guitar playing". The injury was sustained whilst he was playing footy for The Rock Yerong Creek 2nds and his arm was in a sling for a few weeks during which he contributed vocals only whilst Pat, Dick and I carried the music bits! The injury to Woody's finger was permanent and he has played with this disability ever since. Dick's vague, and only memory of playing in the band, was "…didn't someone break their arm?"

Gigs followed at Yerong Creek, St Joseph's and The Klub – this is interesting because nobody can remember this place or even where it might have been situated. This was a two-band gig with The Exits, who later became Blank Cheque - thanks to Peter Quine, their bass player, for this clarification but even he drew a blank on The Klub or where it operated.

Back in action

Tumbarumba Gigs

The band's first gig in Tumbarumba was on the 2nd August., A kindly older lady we knew as Mrs Power used to come down to Wagga and book the band. We would travel up there mid-afternoon and set up our gear early at the show grounds hall, go to one of the local cafes for a hamburger, and then go to Mrs Power's place to shower and change before heading to the gig. Our first trip to Tumbarumba after Jock and Dick joined, turned a bit nasty. Jock, in his previous band, had apparently upset the local blokes when he got too much attention from some of the local girls, and had returned that attention, and the local blokes remembered him.

Probably the night the locals wanted to fight Jock

Some of them ended up on stage at the end of the gig and things looked a bit grim, but we managed to out get of town unscathed. Pat always told the story that one of the locals who had jumped up on the stage, was standing with his arms folded across his very pumped up chest - Pat reckons I suggested to the bloke that he let the air out of his lungs as he was going blue in the face and again, according to Pat, this somewhat deflated the situation although our cars were tailed for some distance after we left town. On another trip to Tumbarumba, I had borrowed my father's new Holden to drive up to the gig. Dick became sick on the way up and said he wouldn't be able to play so he stayed in the car while the rest of the band struggled through the gig minus a proper drummer. Dick smoked whilst laying down across the front seat and unbeknown to him, managed to accidentally drop hot cigarette ash on the plastic seat which caused numerous small burn holes. I copped an earful over this from my father and it was a while before I got the car to go to a gig again!

On another trip up there, Woody hit a sheep in his dad's Morris 1800 in the dark at Ladysmith although the damage did not stop us getting to the gig. Often, in the winter months, the trip home was slow and in heavy fog on the narrow mountain roads, and Pat's FJ did not have the most efficient heating.

Jacky McGrath fills in!

Jacky McGrath was home from Melbourne and on a break from playing either with The Final Four or The Dream in Melbourne, and he had come up with Pat the night Dick got sick. Jacky tried to fill in on drums as best he could, but I remember it was a very long and hard gig to get through without a proper drummer. I think Jock even played drums while Jacky sang a couple of songs. This tended to start feelings with Pat, Woody and I that the band was not really gelling as well at it did with the original blokes from The Rock and whilst Jock was doing a good job on vocals, and Dick's drumming was good, unfortunately it was felt that Dick had let the band down at Tumbarumba. Over the four years I don't remember anyone else not making a gig due to illness – Les, Seymour, Porky and Woody all played despite each carrying football injuries or wearing scars and stitches from the game that day.

> THE MYSTICS have been re-formed and already have a number of engagements. From the line-up one can fairly safely predict that the quality of the sound will be the same as that of the past. The group is Col Moore (vocal), Pat Geaghan (guitar) Woody Finlayson (guitar), Peter Brown bass) and Dennis McGrath (drums).

In the period between the fire at Noah's and when the next band change would occur, apart from a few gigs which were identified from paper ads, memories and/or evidence of any other gigs is very light on despite there being no doubt that the band continued to work consistently notwithstanding that this was also a period when the band did no identified gigs in Wagga. However, another change to band members was about to take place.

The old group back together!

Welcome back!

Ultimately, another change in band members occurred - whether Jock and/or Dick decided to leave or felt pressured to leave, or whether Porky and Seymour approached us with an offer to re-join, or we asked them to come back, no-one can recall. Whatever the reason, the change occurred, was reported in the Youth Beat column on the 7th October, and Jock and Dick left without any remembered drama. It was announced in a paper article that the band had reformed with "Col Moore and Dennis McGrath" returning. Porky purchased a new set of Pearl Drums with Black and White Pearl drum wraps.

There is little information on what Dick did locally after leaving the band – I think he eventually joined The Townsmen and then moved to Sydney, playing briefly in The Delltones [that makes two who played in The Mystics and went on to play in The Delltones]. One of his later gigs was playing drums for Doug Parkinson for about 8 years. Dick now lives on the Central Coast.

Jock, however, moved into a new group but this time it was a three-piece vocal group, The Creations, which was modelled on the Virgil Brothers who were a bit of a hit nationally at the time. The similarity between Jock's group and The Virgil Brothers was that both groups featured three blonde singers in white gear! Pat had a great photo of Jock and his mates on stage at Kyeamba Smith Hall. Another similarity between the two groups was that they both did not last very long! Jock then went solo for a short while – I am not sure if he had a permanent backing group or relied on existing bands. He then moved out of the local music scene. He currently lives in Wonthaggi in Victoria and told me that after moving down that way he did a stint disc-jockeying at functions and was doing a gig at the Collingwood Football Club one night and noticed Julie McGrath, our poster maker from the early days, in the crowd!

The Mystics become Collection

Band names had changed a bit since we started as The Mystics – bands were now often dropping the "The" in front of the name i.e. Traffic, Cream, Procul Harem etc. consequently it was decided that we needed to up-date from The Mystics and "Collection" [not "The Collection"], was chosen as the new name. Unfortunately, some of the dance organisers didn't get the distinction so the band was often advertised under various versions of "Collection".

NAME CHANGE COULD BRING CHANGE OF LUCK FOR GROUP

I can't make up my mind whether Collection should be regarded as a new group.

Actually it is The Mystics—re-formed and re-named—which have been out of action since Noah's was burnt out earlier this year.

Already the group has bookings as far ahead as March next year, although they re-formed, officially, only about four weeks ago.

largely to their fading from the scene for several months. The boys will be talking about this, and their hopes for the future, on

Operating in the old R.S.L. Hall in Baylis Street, Wombat features Captain Walker's Soul and is compered by Groover George

YOUTH PAGE

DON LEONARD'S YOUTH BEAT

The Mystics become Collection – another headline!

This change was the subject of a leading paper article in Don Leonard's Youth Column on the 21st November in which Leonard could not make up his mind if Collection was a new band or not! It was simple – it was version 2 of The Mystics getting back together with a new name! We got a lot of free publicity through Don Leonard's Youth Beat column and this kept the band's name in front of the fans, and the local dance organisers. The Youth Beat column lasted for few years with different journalists and without it, this history would be very much smaller as the articles about the bands have helped to fill gaps in our collective memories. To us, getting a mention in the column was the same as the big city groups getting mentioned in the nationally distributed Go Set magazine.

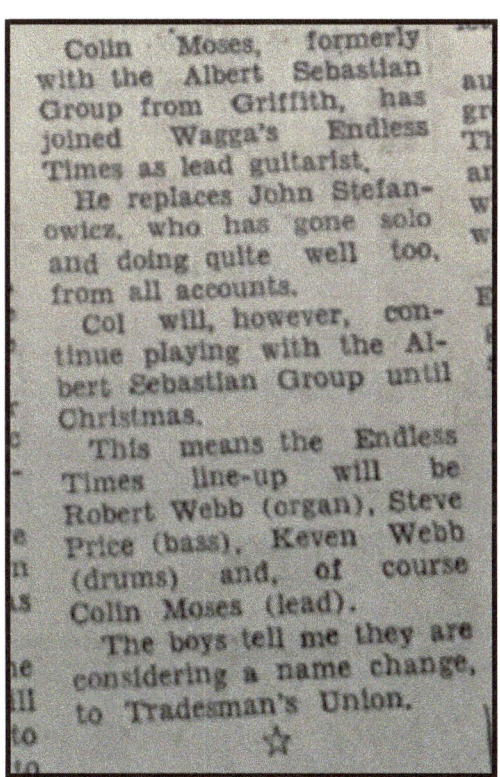

Col Moses – in demand!

Here is an interesting item on the same page as the headlines re change of name – a name that will feature in the next 12 months. Col Moses seems to have got about a bit – prior to this article, Col was in a Leeton group, The Syndicate, and then joined the Albert Sebastian Group in Narrandera, which he appears to have left and, according to this article, joined The Endless Times in Wagga, as a singer/lead guitarist. Col says he never joined The Endless Times and never played lead guitar, so this little snippet seems to be a bit of paper column padding or "bullshit" or both! One of the first gigs Collection played under the new name was at the 2WG Wollundry Room. Notwithstanding that we had deliberately chosen a name without a "The" in front, the band was often advertised as "The" Collection or "The Collections" or just as frustratingly, "Collections"!

A two-band gig with our main rivals and described as Wagga's newest group!

A couple of days later, the band appeared at Kyeamba Smith Hall for Keith Bird in a two-band gig with Captain Walker's Soul [previously Lost and Found] and over the next few weeks, the band played at The Rock, a Wombat dance at the

old RSL Hall next to the Plaza Theatre [don't remember this venue at all], The Rock again, Batlow and for Wombat again, most likely in Tumut. Interestingly, on the 7th December, for the Batlow gig, the band was advertised as The Mystics and on the 14th December, a week later, it was advertised to play a gig at the Boys Club in Tumut as "…the popular Wagga band "The" Collection"! Bookings had obviously been accepted in advance of the name change which had occurred back in October.

No-one can recall how the band handled changes to personnel because in most cases [except for the fire], the band continued playing as booking would have been accepted before any change was possibly known or even anticipated – how long did it take Pat to learn all the numbers we played when Woody took time off notwithstanding that he rehearsed with the band before Woody left - or how long for Woody to get back up to speed with new songs we had added to the song list whilst he was doing his exams? How long did it take Jock to learn our song list when he joined [we probably had a set list of 40 or more songs] – we did have a month off waiting for new gear so he had time to get up to speed before we actually did our first gig a month after the fire. There is no doubt The Mystics would have done songs that The Generation of Love also did so Jock would have had a walk up start with some. Interestingly, I wonder what or whose gear we used waiting for new gear to arrive – did Stan Jones lend us gear in anticipation of a sale? The same comments re Seymour and new songs when he returned to the band in the latter part of 1969. Being out of the band for around five months meant there would have been a few new songs he had to learn, and the change-over of band members took place from one weekend to the next. The drumming parts would have been a bit easier for Dick when he joined, and Porky when he re-joined – they simply had to get the tempo right and add drum fills! Interesting stuff!

The Impacts

Just a side note that when researching the Tumut paper for gig ads, it was incredible how many gigs the local band, The Impacts, did. They were often booked at all dances held in Tumut, Talbingo and Batlow and it's a wonder that The Mystics managed to get any gigs up there due to The Impacts popularity. They were a good band and when Mick Archer arrived on the scene in Tumut and formed Handel's Quartet [first gig on the 8th August 1969] with three members of The Impacts, The Impacts disappeared off the scene for a while. Surprisingly I could only find 7 gigs advertised in the Tumut paper including one for Tumbarumba Showground but on two occasions, both The Mystics and the new Collection did gigs on consecutive weekends in Batlow and Tumut. Batlow seems to have been a little bit of a fan base for both bands and I recall one night when a few of the local girls came backstage after every bracket just to talk with us. This is mirrored by The Mystics and Collection with respect to dances at The Rock – the bands did over 60 identified gigs in the local hall and the Kings Own Hotel. I think the only time other bands were booked to play at The Rock was when The Mystics were already booked elsewhere, and this didn't happen very often as gigs at the hall were generally organised around the availability of the band.

I found gig ads for Lost and Found and The Impacts at The Rock Hall, but only a couple.

Wombat Dances

I am not quite sure when Wombat commenced promoting dances, but most likely sometime towards the end of 1968. The operator, Jimmy Logan, a likeable height-challenged bloke with a limp, would run dances all over the Riverina under the heading of Wombat. He would book a hall or venue, then book a band to play. Jimmy ran dances in Wagga, Tumut, Griffith, Leeton, Tumbarumba and even The Rock at which The Impacts played – but then again, Collection did two Wombat dances in Tumut, The Impacts hometown. Wombat dances in Wagga were usually held in the old RSL Hall next to the Plaza Theatre, but later changed to Kyeamba Smith Hall. I think Jimmy took a leaf out of Keith Bird's operation and varied it by running

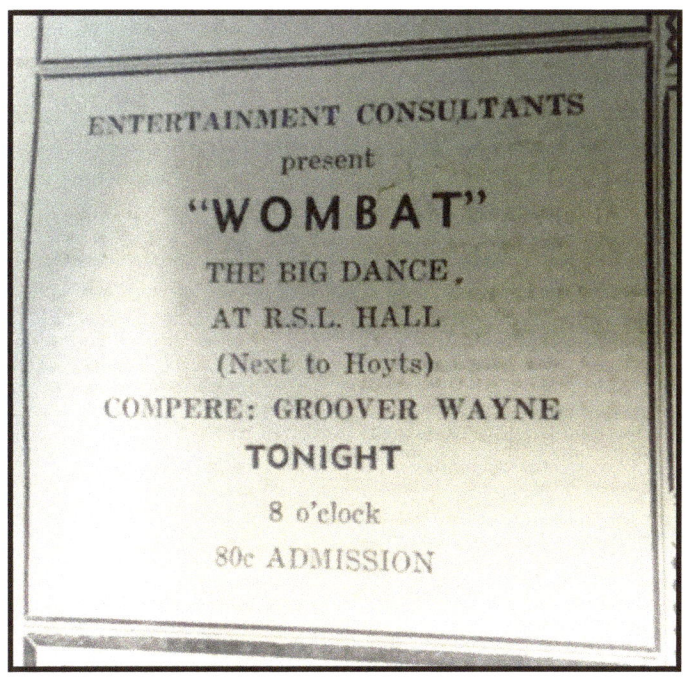

gigs in quite a few towns rather than just Wagga and Griffith, which is where Keith concentrated his dances. The first gig for Wombat was just after the band had changed its name to Collection and a second gig followed soon after. In all, Collection did six gigs for Jimmy, four in Wagga and two in Tumut with four of the gigs being played in 1969. As an added attraction, Groover Wayne from 2WG, would compere the dances and play records between brackets.

Keith Bird had moved to Sydney in mid-1969, and whilst he was still running dances, now under the name of Pacesetter, he was easing out of dance promotion consequently Kyeamba Smith Hall became more available. Keith had also handed over the running of his dances in Griffith to a local bloke and basically ended up totally out of the scene around early 1970 or not long after.

Seymour leaves again

Despite his decision to return to the band in October, Seymour was again under pressure due to work on the family farm and he decided that he would have to leave the band once and for all - he had only been back for a couple of months. Again, we were looking for a singer and not long after Seymour's announcement, Pat turned up at Moore's woolshed for a rehearsal with a bloke called Col "Uncle Col" Moses. He would be the fourth singer for the band since the beginning of the year!

Collection and The Impacts in each other's stamping ground!

Col "Uncle Col" [Unc] Moses

Uncle Col [Unc] was from Leeton and had been an original member of The Syndicate, a band formed in Leeton. He then joined the Albert Sebastian Group, out of Narrandera, and around the same time had moved to Wagga for work reasons but the resultant travelling back to the Narrandera/Leeton/Griffith area each weekend to meet gig commitments with the Narrandera band became a drag so Unc decided to look to joining a band in Wagga.

Coincidentally, Pat and Unc were in Stan Jones' music shop on a Saturday morning, probably late November or early December and Unc's memory is that Stan Jones introduced him to Pat. It was during discussion that Pat mentioned we were looking for a new singer. Unc, maybe remembering seeing The Mystics at Subway/Noahs earlier in the year, indicated an interest. Pat said he very quickly made some enquiries about Unc through a couple of his former band mates and they gave him a wrap, so Pat invited him to our next rehearsal at Moore's woolshed. Whilst no-one can clearly remember what songs we tried, Unc passed the test and he was welcomed into the band. The actual date is unclear although I am reasonably certain Unc started rehearsing with Collection around mid-December however, the very first mention in the paper that he had joined Collection didn't appear until the 30th January 1969. Again, a milestone event for the band is not remembered by anyone with any sort of certainty. It is most likely that Unc did not start performing with the band until January. The weekly Youth Beat feature in the paper ceased around mid-December and didn't resume until late January. Consequently, any news relating to bands in December was not going to be reported until late January when the column resumed.

> FORMER ALBERT Sebastian Group singer, Colin Moses, has joined The Collection, which has 12 months work lined up at the Kings Own Hotel, The Rock . . .

Unc joins a band called "The" Collection!

Christmas Eve Dance

As per previous years, the band was booked to do the traditional dance at The Rock Hall, this time with Porky sober and it being either the last, or second last, gig for Seymour. Again, an important band date in that an original member was leaving the band permanently, but no-one remembers it at all!

New Year's Eve

I could not find an advertised gig ad for the band on New Year's Eve, which is a bit surprising as all bands would work that night because of the number of dances and functions organised to see in the New Year. However, there are a couple of photos which were taken at the Wagga Country Club of The Mystics, with Seymour out front and by the way the punters are dressed, it seems to have been a special night! This has raised some question as to whether the dance was a New Year's Eve gig or, in fact, a private function such as a 21st birthday. I tend to lean towards it being New Year's Eve for a Batchelor's and Spinster's/Leaf Turner's-type dance, where, as previously highlighted, attendance was by invitation only consequently no paper ads. It is reasonable to assume that the band had a booking for New Year's Eve, a night when every band worked. By extension, I believe this then means that Seymour's last gig was this gig on New Year's Eve. In further support of this assumption, I have a definite recall of playing a gig one night at the Country Club and always have associated it with a New Year's Eve gig. My recollection is that a dance was also being held at the Wagga Boat Club the same night and punters walked between the two venues. My recollections also include being told about female underwear being found discarded along the path between the two venues which suggests that it took some of the punters a bit longer to get from one venue to the other!

During the year, the band played at The Rock only 5 identified times, which was a big reduction over previous years. The Swimming Pool Committee appears to have reduced or even stopped the number of dances run and at the same time, the band was getting more gigs in Wagga which included the short-lived residency at Subway and Noahs for 3 months at the beginning of the year. The Noah's fire put the band out of business for about a month and most likely, because of that, bookings did not start to come in until it was apparent that the band was up and running again. Additionally, the Gig Guide shows a substantial drop off in the number of gigs generally. The band did gigs at Lockhart and Tumbarumba on a regular basis but cannot be confirmed due to the unavailability of papers to access and identify gig ads. It is reasonable to assume that the band was still in demand with gigs at The Rock, Tumbarumba, Henty and Lockhart.

Seymour's last night? - New Year's Eve at the Wagga Country Club

Up to this point, none of the band had let their hair grow to any length – Pat, Woody, Porky and I all styled our hair in the Beatle fashion but as we all had day jobs and long hair had generally not yet been accepted in the regions, we remained a neatly conservative band in that respect. Seymour, on the other hand, had very curly hair and he had it cut quite short because it would have looked crap if he ever let it grow!

Gigs for the Year

The band played 4 gigs in January, and only 2 in February plus a 3-piece gig because Seymour and I were on holidays in New Zealand. There were 5 gigs in March, none identified in early April including Noah's – two other bands were booked to play the first two weekends of April, The Gingerbread Men from Melbourne and St Pete Florida Movement, a new local band, and I suspect this was because Jock had joined the band and we needed to rehearse with him. After the fire, the band started again in May playing 1 gig, 2 in June and 3 in August – this period is very lean for identified gigs but the band would have still have had some advanced bookings prior to Seymour leaving and also would have started to be booked once it was known that it was up and running. Again, evidence of gigs simply has not been found but Jock's memory, as vague as it is to specific gigs, is that the band was working reasonably consistently. Likewise, only 2 gigs for September and none in October which would simply not be correct – the band would have been playing but the gigs were most likely out of Wagga and could not be identified. November produced 4 gigs and December 4. It is disappointing that so many gigs have not been able to be identified because the popularity of the band would have ensured that it worked consistently despite the fire setback in May and the changes in band members. Had Woody been able to locate his 1968 diary, it would have closed the gaps in gigs!

1969

Unc fitted in straight away and brought with him an added benefit - a band trailer which carried all the gear. The band would now be formally based out of Wagga as Pat, Unc and Woody were all Wagga-based along with all the gear. Porky and I would travel into Wagga in his Morris 1100S and join the others before heading off to gigs in Unc's car with the trailer in tow.

Unc's inclusion added to the professionalism and playing standard which allowed the band to move into more complex songs and harmonies. From memory, the song list was constantly being added to and Pat was starting to take songs off albums rather than simply relying on the Top 40.

The start of a 4-month residency.

The New Year saw the band enter into an agreement to play a regular weekly gig on a Saturday night at The Kings Own Hotel at The Rock starting on the 18th January – another residency. The publican, Harry Pill, had been putting on high class Tivoli-type shows with showgirls and other acts from Sydney for quite some time and as this had come to an end, he wanted to keep the customers coming in on a Saturday night. Harry knew Porky and I very well because he was the president of the footy club and as we were first grade players, we were highly regarded by him.

Interestingly, the following article appeared in the Youth Beat column on the 16th January and suggests that the re-united Mystics, now Collection, will be playing at The Kings Own Hotel – this is not correct because it suggests that Seymour was still in the band in the middle of January 1969, when Collection started its residency at the pub. I believe that he had left the band at the end of 1968 and he never did a gig at the hotel.

This little bit is not correct!

Those embarrassing shirts - Unc's introduction to joining Collection

I think to start with, we simply wore our normal band gear but unfortunately, in her misguided effort to keep the Sydney show-girl type atmosphere happening, Kath Pill had shirts made for each of us that were based on a South American Mardi Gras-style design with multi-coloured ruffled sleeves with a different colour in the body of the shirt. We hated them but it was part of the gig, so we had no option but to wear them – the shirts simply did not go with a band playing Top 40 pop and rock songs. The photos are rather hazy, but the cause of our embarrassment is obvious. One night I can remember a visitor to the pub, filming us with a small movie camera as we played – I was not sure whether he thought they looked great or was taking a movie to show his mates for a good laugh. According to the paper, we had secured a 12 months residency with the hotel, but it appears that these nights lasted for about four months only. The band ended up doing 14 gigs at the pub and Porky's memory is that we always drew a good crowd despite the shirts, which would have made our embarrassment somewhat bearable.

> IT APPEARS THAT The Collection's luck is still not with them all the way ... but this time the morale is and the group is determined to make it.
>
> Despite a number of problems, the group put up a fair showing in Wagga on Saturday night, and are determined to continue to improve.
>
> Their own re-arrangement of a classical number really went over well.
>
> The Collection has jobs lined up for Wagga, The Rock, Tumut and Tumbarumba.

At this time, Pat had been teaching himself clarinet and he debuted the instrument at the pub. His "masterpiece" was an instrumental version of the old standard, "I'm in the mood for love", played early in the night along with other instrumentals – a number which probably enhanced the "show-style" shirts we were wearing.

I wonder what the problems were? - and "The classical number" was a hit!

> This week's mail included a letter from Tumbarumba which read:
>
> "One Wagga group which is proving very popular with the fans in Tumbarumba is Collection.
>
> "They have made about six appearances in the town in the past six or eight months, first as the Mystics and later as Collection.
>
> "Each time they seem to be better than the time before, and would compare favourably with many of the big name groups in capital cities."

Pat also used the clarinet in a Donovan song around at the time which featured the instrument. For something a bit different, Pat had also arranged a guitar version of "The Hall of the Mountain King" - he always said that Porky did a really great job on this number. The previous item from the Youth Beat column makes mention of "a classical" number by the band going over very well at a dance in Wagga in late 1968. In February, the Youth Beat column in the Daily Advertiser mentioned a letter received from a fan in Tumbarumba saying that Collection was very popular in the town and that the popularity went back to The Mystics as well. The letter also stated that, in the opinion of the writer, the group compared favourably with big-name groups from the capital cities!

Some nice comments from an unknown fan

Mullengandra [Holbrook] B&S Ball

The band was booked to play at the Mullengandra Hall, between Holbrook and Albury, on the last day in February. It was big night and the band went over particularly well. It was a well-paid gig because, the band was also booked for the recovery the next night at the same venue. Woody's diary notes that the band was paid $180 – not sure if this was just for the ball or was for both nights. Anyway, two gigs without moving the gear would have been appreciated. I have a faint recollection that the organisers paid for the band to stay at a local motel on the Friday night.

Groover Wayne - the DJ

Groover Wayne came to 2WG from Victoria and really got the scene going in terms of promotion of local bands and the local musical scene. He interviewed bands on his radio show in the afternoon on a Thursday and Collection was interviewed a couple of times – all great promotion! He also took up DJing at Wombat dances however he eventually left 2WG and ended up at 2SM in Sydney as one of the "good guys" and really made a name for himself in the Sydney radio market. He died prematurely in 1992.

Groover Wayne - the Roadie

Wayne "Groover" Black, who worked at the same business as Unc, appeared with him at his first rehearsal with Collection at Moore's woolshed. He would come to most of the gigs and help us as a roadie although we still did a lot of the setting and packing up as well. Groover was a nice bloke and did all this for nothing – I don't think we ever discussed paying him to help us even though he did it without us specifically requesting him to be a roadie.

A novel idea

Around late February we must have discussed the possibility of doing something a bit different i.e. getting work on a cruising ship.

An official response!

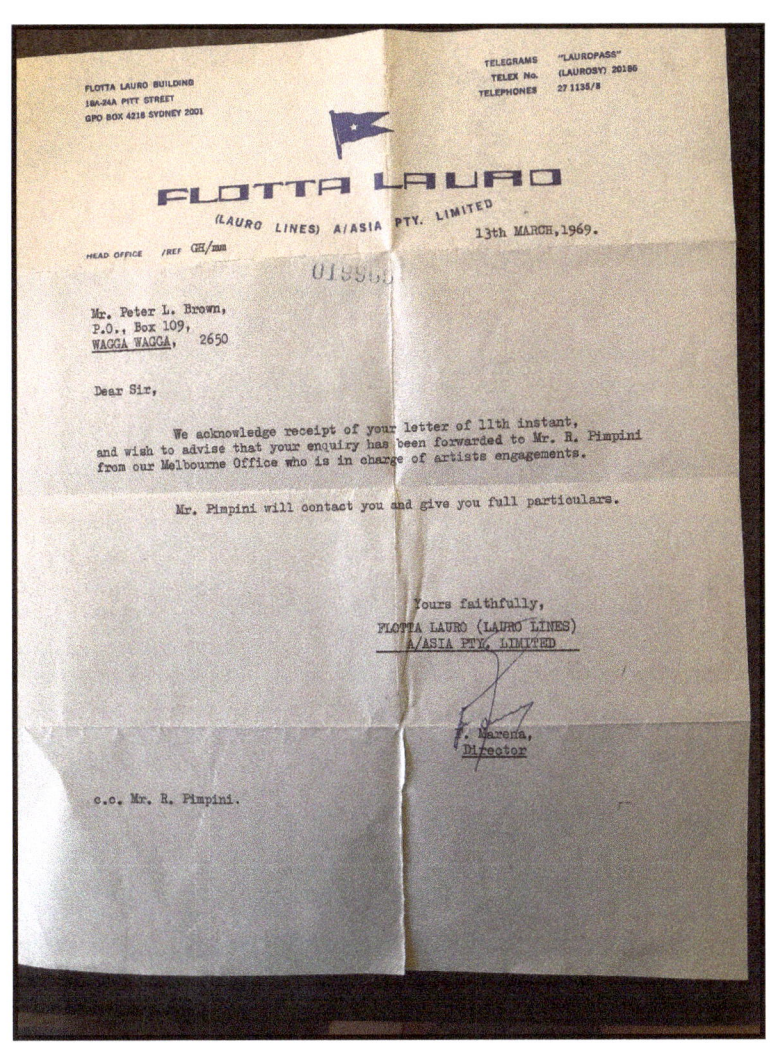

As can be seen from the letter here, I had written to Flotta Lauro, an Italian shipping company, who had offices in Sydney, as well as writing to a couple of other shipping lines. In the general letter to each, I set out our band's experience and as well said we were versatile and could play different styles of music including jazz. I think I included this genre because Pat was playing clarinet, but I obviously did not enunciate that he knew only one song from the jazz era. I eventually received replies from each shipping company and from memory, at least one said they would put our name onto their list of entertainers, but I received no further correspondence from them. The others, whilst polite in their reply, basically said they were already booked for the season and we left it at that.

Book Book Hall Ball [again]

The band again played for the Book Book Tennis Club in the Book Book Hall. This night is only memorable because the bloke who broke his arm dancing to the band the previous year was again in attendance and came out into the side room the band was using between brackets to have a chat. He was sitting on a wooden benchtop whilst he was talking with us and when he slid off to leave, he tore the arse out of his very nice dinner suit pants. He told us that he would never again go to any dance we played at – he reckoned we were bad luck. Many years later, the hall burnt down and was never rebuilt.

The band continued to work every Saturday night at The Kings Own Hotel as well as playing gigs at Lockhart and Batlow. In fact, the band played 5 gigs at the Lockhart RSL Hall Supper Room, one of them on a Thursday night, between the end of February and the start of April indicating that Collection was very much in demand by the organisers and/or the fans, and had re-established the band in that town after the initial popularity of The Mystics in 1966 and 1967.

The ties are off so it must have been hot

The After 5 Club

Despite Unc having no memory of the gig [nor any of us], Collection played at the After 5 on the 6th April, the band's one and only appearance for the year at the venue. It was a two-band gig with the Tin Soldiers, led by Rick Dawson and included Nick Freeman on drums [**see Not the Final Chapter**]. It appears by this time that the After 5 Club had lost its popularity as I could not find too many more gig ads for this great venue.

The band also did gigs at the Broadway Theatre in Junee and for the first time, at the Teacher's College campus near the Wagga Showgrounds. The College gigs were always great gigs as we were playing to people who were all about our age and they appreciated our style of music.

> Soldiers . . . . Col Moses doing well with the Collection . . . . Pat Geaghan on another "fly-by-night" guest spot . . . . Peter

Unc doing well and Pat playing elsewhere

Unc's First Gig at The Rock Hall

As the band had been playing Saturdays regularly at The Kings Own Hotel at The Rock during the residency from the beginning of the year, it wasn't until May that the band was booked to play a gig at the hall, the original stamping ground of The Mystics. In fact, the band only did three gigs for 1969 at the hall and one of these was captured in a photo showing Unc fronting the band in old familiar surroundings for Porky, Woody and me. There are a couple of photos showing me singing, generally with Woody at the same mike – Woody never left me in

Unc at The Rock Hall with two tone hair or wearing a flat cap! – and me singing into Woody's right ear, which he would have really appreciated!

any doubt that he was not a fan of my singing! I can't imagine why! Maybe it has something to do with my old boarding-school teacher's assessment of my vocal ability!

Porky on his own – often left out of photos of the band when playing!

Over the next couple of weeks, the band did a fair bit of travelling out of Wagga. There were two gigs in consecutive weeks at the Batlow Institute in Batlow, one at Holbrook, and one at Tumut for Wombat, all Friday gigs plus Kyeamba Smith Hall twice. Batlow was always a good place to play and the band was well received probably because the Impacts did a lot of work in the area and Collection were probably seen as a good change for the local punters. As well, gigs at the Broadway Theatre and St. Joseph's made it a very full month for the band. The band's final gig at The Kings own was on the 10th May.

As was the case since the band originally formed, Porky and I were still playing 1st Grade footy with The Rock. Generally, we were lucky, and injuries never stopped us playing but during one game at Temora in May, Porky got hammered and ended up at the Temora hospital.

The day Porky got hammered playing footy – and we still played well!

I had to wait while they stitched him up then it was a mad dash from Temora to the Holbrook gig [about 160 kilometres] in Porky's Mini. According to the paper, it was a great night and the band went over very well. In May, the band played 10 gigs for the month, making it the second heaviest gig month. Clearly, the band was in demand.

30th May 1969 - a very important date

For quite some time, I had noticed from afar, a very attractive girl who worked in a dress shop across the street from where I worked – I found out her name was June through our office tea lady who happened to be her aunty. Earlier in the year I had purchased a brand new car, my first, so one afternoon after work, I waited in my new Torana on the street where I knew she walked home and as she came past, I jumped out of the car and introduced myself and offered her a ride home, which she accepted. I think she knew my face from seeing me around her workplace, but she didn't know my name. I told her we were playing at St Joseph's on Friday night, the 30th May, and asked her to come and see the band! When she told her older sister who had given her a ride home, her sister said I had a reputation for being "…the hottest thing in town", meaning that I had reputedly had plenty of girlfriends – the fact was quite the opposite – I had not had a girlfriend for a couple of years and even that one was hardly serious stuff! On the Friday night, she brought a couple of friends with her to St Joseph's and I spoke with her and her friends

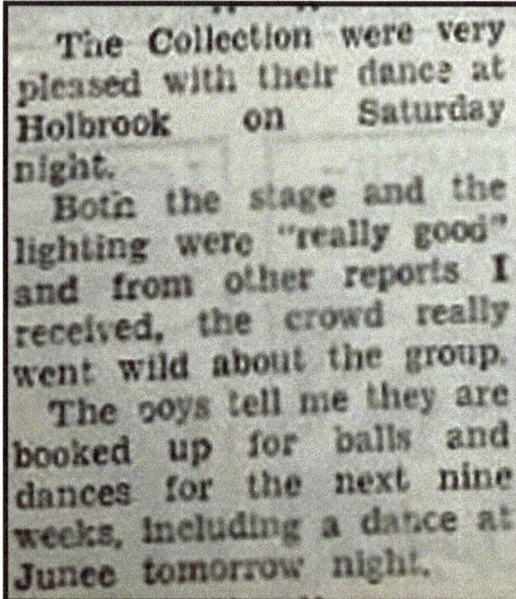

A very important gig – for me!

between one of the brackets but they left not long after – I think it was simply they had already planned to go somewhere else that night – but she did turn up and we have been together virtually ever since.

As can be seen from the Gig Guide, June was the heaviest month for bookings since the band started with ten gigs which kicked off with a three-gig weekend - at St Joseph's Friday night, and Kyeamba Smith Hall on Saturday - both venues were becoming regular bookings for the band - and the weekend finished on Sunday night with a Keith Bird gig at Griffith. It was a long and late trip home after the gig and getting up to go to work the next day would have been a drag.

The second weekend was also a three-gig weekend with gigs at Junee, Wagga RSL and Gregadoo. The Saturday and Sunday night gigs were for the ANZ Bank weekend which was an annual weekend for ANZ staff from all over. These gigs were still being held years later when Duke, a band that Pat and I formed and played in between 1978 – 82, played

I suppose "Conservative" was reasonable - but the music wasn't!

this gig a couple of times as well! The next weekend saw the band playing at the Wagga Batchelor's and Spinster's Ball at Kyeamba Smith Hall on the Friday night. On this night, the paper took photos of the band in new suits, which had been ordered through Warren Glanville's Menswear shop. The suits, brown woollen extra length coats and matching pants with lime green shirts and a variety of ties was set off by what we termed Donald Duck boots, in a tan colour – because they had a sort of spats finish with small buttons. They should have been called Uncle Scrooge boots because he was the one who wore spats in the Donald Duck comics! The band looked very professional. The following week, the Daily Advertiser included a photo together with an article about the band. Since January, the band had played three different B&S type balls or similar functions.

The following week, the band played the Teacher's College Ball on the Friday night, which was mentioned in the Youth Beat column as one of the best gigs the band had played at, and again at Holbrook on the Saturday, this time without Porky suffering any injuries. With very consistent and constant work, the band's sound and playing had gone up a couple of notches!

The Collection Sign

Pat made up a tall wooden illuminated sign [can't remember if it was a flashing sign or not] with the word "Collection" cut out of the sides and it was used on the stage to advertise the band. I think it was made for the Battle of the Bands contest we were about to take part in as I remember us working on it the Saturday afternoon before the band contest when I should have been playing football [I used an excuse that I was sick and therefore couldn't play that day] – Porky was already out injured so he had an excuse. Pat said it was previously a sign he had made for The End and he had changed it to

The "Collection" sign beside Pat at a St. Joseph's gig!

Collection – from memory, it was a dead weight! July kicked off with a three-gig weekend – Junee Friday, Kyeamba Smith Saturday and the Battle of the Sounds on Sunday.

The Battle of the Sounds

The band contest was organised by 2WG and was held at the Civic Theatre in Wagga on the 6th July as part of the Hoadley's National Battle of the Sounds contest which was held in every state. We entered because we were quietly confident that we had a very good chance of winning, which I suppose all the other groups did as well. Each band had to do two or three numbers – Pat had arranged a Beatles medley and as well, we did "Eloise" by Barry Ryan, a big song that went for over 5 minutes – not normal at the time. Porky remembers that we played well but Collection ended up running third behind a band from the local College of Advanced Education, Nanna's Passion Poem [Porky christened them Nana's Passion Pit] - they were generally ordinary but had a good lead guitarist who carried them. They went on to the Canberra final and bombed but the lead guitarist got a special mention which made it quite apparent that he stood out from the rest of the band because their lack of musical ability only heightened his ability. Blank Cheque, who came second, were quite a good group and threw confetti over the crowd as part of their stage act, trying to stand out from the other competing bands and it appears the judges liked this. There were three judges and each one came up with a different winner. There was a lot of disgruntled punters with the decision [as reported in the paper a week later - see next page] so we were the best in one judge's opinion but lost on account of us having no stage show – we just stood there and played as we always did. We were shattered as we felt we were by far the best sounding band on the day and the battle was to find the best sounding band, not the best stage show. In fact, I don't recall any local bands at the time having any sort of stage act which was used at a gig – we all just simply got up on stage and played. There

On stage at the Battle of the Sounds – a disappointing result

was also a suggestion that the only female judge, who worked for the Daily Advertiser and was now writing the Youth Column in the paper, voted against us as a pay-back because we had not taken her seriously when she came to do an interview with the band at Unc's flat one Sunday afternoon - the interview never made the Youth Beat page.

The following week, the Youth Beat Column carried the following article about the decision from the band contest which had taken place the previous week. Clearly, the punters were not happy with the judge's decision and Collection could take some heart from this reaction because the punters wouldn't react if the best band won. There was no doubt in our mind that we were miles better than the winning

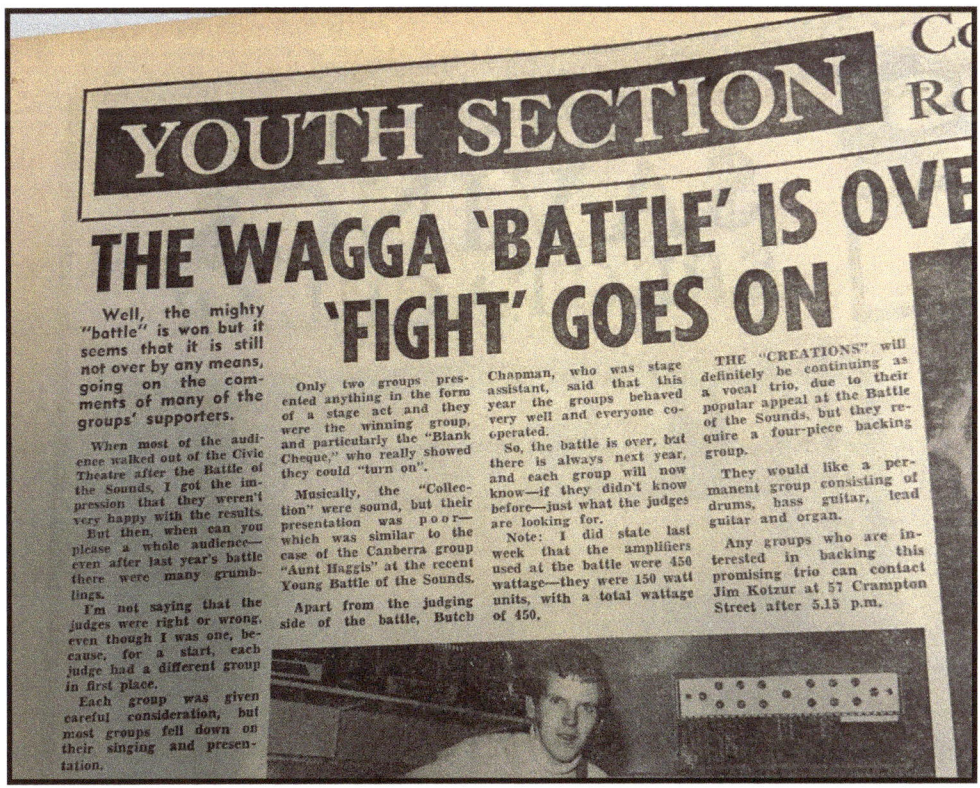

"The Wagga "Battle" is over, but the "fight goes on"
The reaction to the judge's decision for the Battle of the Sounds – Peter
Quine, bass player for Blank Cheque is featured in the photo

group although band suits would have given a conservative appearance as opposed to Nanna's Passion "Pit" who looked more "hip" and like a band from Woodstock. I can't remember how Blank Cheque were dressed [whether in a uniform or not] so I suppose they also felt a bit cheated as well. The article says that most groups "fell down on singing and presentation". The number of gigs Collection had been playing, and the rehearsals the band did weekly, would suggest that our sound and playing would have been tight so I expect the writer's comments to be more about justification for "her" opinion than any suggestion that she/they might have got it wrong! I am not sure what "presentation" the writer of the column expected – our suits looked smart and after all these years, we still believe our musical ability and sound was ahead of the rest.

Unc's Wagga Flat

Unc had rented a flat at the bottom end of Fitzmaurice Street next to a service station. The flat was on the first floor of the building and entry was gained by a set of rear external stairs. There was a suggestion that the building had been a brothel during the War. The flat had a big lounge area, small kitchen, two bedrooms and a small bathroom and a balcony over the street footpath. We used the place as a rehearsal venue which generally took place on a Sunday afternoon after the Friday and Saturday gigs. We often crashed there after Sat night and it was a common thing to head up to the Dragon Chinese Restaurant for a Sunday lunch of fried rice with sweet and sour sauce – George Young, the owner, also made the best curried prawns and rice. The flat became a bit of a meeting place and people often ended up there after gigs or called in over the weekend.

Because Unc's flat had become a base for the band, Porky and I used to stay there at times, sometimes getting the only spare bed or sleeping on the lounge. On the nights we didn't and during the drive home in the early hours of the morning to The Rock in his Mini, Porky would often turn his headlights off, and we would be driving along the Olympic Highway in the dark. He would wait for an oncoming car to appear then switch the lights back on as the oncoming car got nearer – it must have frightened the crap out of the other driver, but we thought it was a pisser. His other trick was to pretend to let the hand brake off about half-way home to The Rock – small things amuse small minds – it never failed to seem hilarious!

After Gigs

The Crown Corner café, owned by a Greek family, was on the corner of Fitzmaurice and Kincaid Streets [now Unique Coffee Shop] quite close to Unc's flat and was the go-to place after any in-town or out-of-town gig – a hamburger, steak sandwich or mixed grill at about 2am or later was always the go. All the bands used to call in. Daisy's Diner, which was situated in Dobney Avenue, was also a haunt of bands after gigs - I think it operated only for about 12-18 months. It was a convenient eating place late at night for Porky and I as we passed the place heading home to The Rock when we didn't stay at Unc's flat.

The Ungrateful Fan

Around this time, a girl from Tumut lobbed at the flat late one Saturday night – she had come down to a gig we played at and had missed her ride home. No-one remembers how she found us at Unc's flat but there was no way she was going to get home that night, so she slept on the lounge. The next day she wanted us to find her a ride back home so we contacted 2WG and asked if they could put a call out over the radio for anyone travelling to Tumut, but they had no response – in the end, after we had finished a rehearsal, Pat took Jock McKenzie with him, and drove to Tumut in his FJ which would have taken him well over two hours to complete and she didn't bother to even thank him when he delivered her home! The band must have played out of town over the next couple of weeks but again returned to Wagga to play St Josephs on Saturday night and an afternoon concert at the Teacher's College on the Sunday.

The Broadway Theatre, Junee

> Wagga will have its first big pop concert in just two weeks time.

> Among the groups are "Handel Quartet," from Tumut, "Blank Cheque," "Collection," "Tin Soldiers," "Rampance Rant," "Spiritual Feeling," "Coloured Rain" and the "Tourist Brothers."

Tommy Waugh, a likeable bloke of Asian descent, started to book the band for gigs in the old Junee picture house, the Broadway Theatre. He had two daughters who were very attractive, and both were wrapt in the band. Between April and August, Collection played five gigs for Tommy and the band started to get a following in the town.

In August, Collection played a gig at a Big BBQ and Dance at the Downside Hall as well as the Wagga High School Ball which would have been in the auditorium at the High School. On the 15th August, the band played for a Youth Rally at Kyeamba Smith Hall and it was reported in the paper that around 1000 kids were expected to attend. On the Sunday, the band was again back at Kyeamba Smith Hall for a concert which was being held, as a fund raiser for one of the Miss Wagga entrants.

Sunday Pop Concert – Kyeamba Smith Hall

This involved eight bands and some vocal acts including Jock McKenzie, who had left The Creations after a short stint and was now going solo as a new musical direction, backed by Blank Cheque. I remember this was the first gig we saw Mick Archer ex-The Shantines, ex-The Final Four, ex-The Dream, since he had lobbed back in Wagga. His band was Handel's Quartet and included some good Tumut

On stage at the Broadway Theatre, Junee, the night we took the girls! Photos of the band show that Woody and I held our guitars at the same angle!

musos who had been in The Impacts, and who had recently broken up. They did a great version of Procul Harem's "Whiter Shade of Pale", which included Mick on keyboards even though he was a drummer. According to the paper, attendance at this free pop concert was ordinary and the Youth Column lamented the lack of interest and support shown despite all the bands offering their services without cost and for a good cause.

The month finished off with two gigs at The Broadway Theatre, Junee, one being a regular dance and the other, a ball where we took the girlfriends because it must have been a two-band gig. The band also played at Ganmain which was reported as being a great night. Finishing off the month, another gig at the Downside Hall which was again well attended. The Junee ball gig is memorable because of a photo taken of the band that night with the girls, a copy of which surfaced for the Reunion Concert in 2005, and which had been edited with respect to Woody and his partner! Interestingly, three of the girls in the photograph eventually became wives. For some unexplained reason, Woody's choice of partner seems to have been roundly rejected by someone subsequently viewing the photo and the following comparison photos have been included to see if the reader can see the subtle editing which has taken place.

You really need a keen eye, but can you spot the edit in the bottom photo!

Voted Wagga's Top Group

Late in August, the Wagga Wagga Progress, a free paper which had been around for many years, conducted a survey of young people in Wagga at a St Joseph's dance on various topics, one question being their preferred band – and Collection topped the poll by a good margin. At that time there would have been about a dozen groups in Wagga, so the popularity win was a big thing for Collection. In all, both bands played seven gigs at St Joseph's Hall and was without doubt, the favoured bands at this venue. During my research through the Wagga Daily Advertiser, other bands played gigs at St Joey's but not with the consistency that The Mystics and Collection did. Notwithstanding the results of the Battle of the Sounds in July, the band was now, by popular vote, Wagga's top group. Unfortunately, the article headline includes "The Collection" rather than simply our proper name, "Collection"! The following week, an article appeared about the band in the next edition following an interview with Pat. September kicked off with gigs at Griffith on a Friday night and Tumbarumba on the Saturday night – we travelled 600+ miles in two nights! More gigs during the month included the band playing at St. Josephs, and at Wesley Hall Cabaret and Coffee Shop, which was in the hall beside the Wesley Church on the corner of Tarcutta and Johnson Streets.

"The" Collection! – another headline! Says much about a "Third" at The Battle of the Sounds the previous month

Myall Park Hall B&S

The band was booked to play at Myall Park for a B&S ball – the hall was in the middle of nowhere somewhere near Griffith. Rainfall readings for the Riverina in 1969 showed they were the highest on record. When we arrived at the hall, the ground was so wet that the band car and trailer could not be driven into the hall site because the surrounds were water-logged so we had to leave the car and trailer parked on the side of the sealed road and carry all the gear over a fence, across muddy ground and into the hall. The ball made the social pages in a Sydney paper the next week and the band got a mention.

Unc and Pat - another B&S type gig

In the middle of the month, the band played its first gig at the Wesley Cabaret Room in the Johnson Street Hall next to the Wesley Church, and Kyeamba Smith the next night. Following the Wesley Cabaret gig, the band was approached to take part in a special Youth Church Service which was to be held on a Sunday night This was a first for any band in Wagga and the church service drew a very large crowd from the city and places around. As can be seen from the photo, the band was squeezed into a very small space which necessitated one of the amps, next to the pulpit, having to be tilted forward so Porky could get in behind the amps to his drums. The band played three songs at different times during the service which meant Porky squeezing in behind the amps each time – during one of these, Woody tilted his amp to let Porky get past but he was too quick putting the amp back in position and managed to trap Porky's foot between his amp and the pulpit– he was left hopping on one leg until Woody woke up and tilted the amp so Porky could get his foot free. A bit of light unrehearsed entertainment for the church punters!

Pop group for service

A Wagga pop group will be featured during a youth service in the Wagga Methodist Church next Sunday night.

The group, "The Collection," will play several ballad-type numbers, replacing the usual choir for this part of the service.

It is the first time that a pop group has been invited to play at an evening service in the church, the supervising minister, the Rev. K. A. Brooks, said yesterday.

He said it was hoped the appearance of the group would be an additional attraction to Wagga's youth.

Guest preacher at the service will be a "younger minister," the Rev. Ian Diamond, of Lake Cargelligo.

The service starts at 7.30 p.m. and will probably be attended by young people from Junee and Lockhart, as well as Wagga.

The "youth services" are held once a month and are popular with the church's young people.

Collection in church – a first for Wagga, a first for the band and probably for a couple in the band, as well!

plans are some... the air" at the moment.

So, the pop scene will only be left with the "Collection" and the "Spiritual Feeling"—and even the "Collection" will probably be a different group as there could be some change in members shortly.

Hint of a change!

During October, the band played out of town gigs at Griffith and Ganmain and on a Sunday at Kyeamba Smith Hall. In a Youth Beat column early in the month, it was reported that there was a hint of a pending change in the band. Both Porky and I must have dropped some hints that we were going to finish up.

The report was part of an article lamenting the number of groups which had broken up in the latter part of the year and that Collection would be one of two groups still standing, despite the suggestion of a change in the band make-up.

Listed gigs for November were for Wombat in Wagga, another at Wesley Cabaret Room, The Rock Hall and the Tumbarumba Showgrounds. There were virtually no identified gigs from the 19th October until the first week in November. Considering the consistency of the band from the beginning of the year, it is hard to accept that over the three weekends in this period, the band did not play at all - the band was most likely playing in towns well outside Wagga's advertising radius. One reason for the low gig numbers in November was that the band had two weeks off from the middle of month because of a very special occasion.

Unc gets married

Unc and Denitsa tied the knot on the 15th November and the wedding was held in Leeton with the reception at the Hydro Hotel, an historic old hotel in the town – Denitsa had worked for the owners. It was a great day and all the band attended, with girlfriends – the day was made more memorable for me as my parents had purchased a specially tailored three-piece pin-striped suit for my 21st birthday back in August and this was one of the first occasions it was making an appearance.

As I was leaving home to drive to Leeton, I grabbed my new suit, which was hanging in my wardrobe, put it in the car and headed off with my girlfriend, June. We had booked rooms at the Hydro and when I was getting ready, to my horror, I discovered that the new suit pants weren't on the hanger with the new coat and waist-coat – they were still hanging on a separate hanger at home. Despite it being quite warm, I had fortunately decided to wear a pair of long flared pants instead of shorts for the trip over – so I went to the wedding wearing a two tone outfit – dark grey pin-striped coat and waist coat, and light grey striped flared pants, and I thought it looked pretty cool!

Keith Bird's Withdrawal from the Music Scene

Keith had been very successful and whenever he brought big groups or singers to town, he would get Don Leonard to interview them for his Youth Beat column in the paper as part of his overall promotion. He said Leonard, despite getting access to some of Australia's top groups and pop stars through Keith, started to write negative reports about the dances and mentioned "drugs" in an article which had an immediate impact on the numbers turning up to Keith's dances. Keith complained to Leonard over the articles and went on local TV and into the local paper, refuting that drugs were a part of the scene "inside" the dances, and that he had no influence over what went on "outside". Whilst he said that he always employed security people at dances unfortunately his promotion business started to suffer with decreasing crowd numbers, so he eventually pulled the pin on the business and moved to Sydney in 1969 and although he did run a couple of dances from Sydney, he finally ceased his dance promotion business.

Pat turned 21 in November and on his birthday or thereabouts, despite never having an alcoholic drink since he joined the band, or forever for that matter, decided to demonstrate that he could drink a can of beer faster than any other band member – none of us accepted the challenge but Pat still downed the can in pretty fast time - the only time any of us had ever witnessed him drink anything other than Coke.

Around this time, the band played a big gig at the Wagga Airport in an aircraft hangar for the Young National Party organisation from The Rock. From a vague memory, I think that the night had some reference to a Snoopy and the Red Baron night. I could not find an ad for this which is odd because it was such a big gig and a first time that a dance was held in an aircraft hangar but as it was being put on by a junior political party, it was probably a "blue bloods" event and therefore by invitation only - but it still attracted a large crowd.

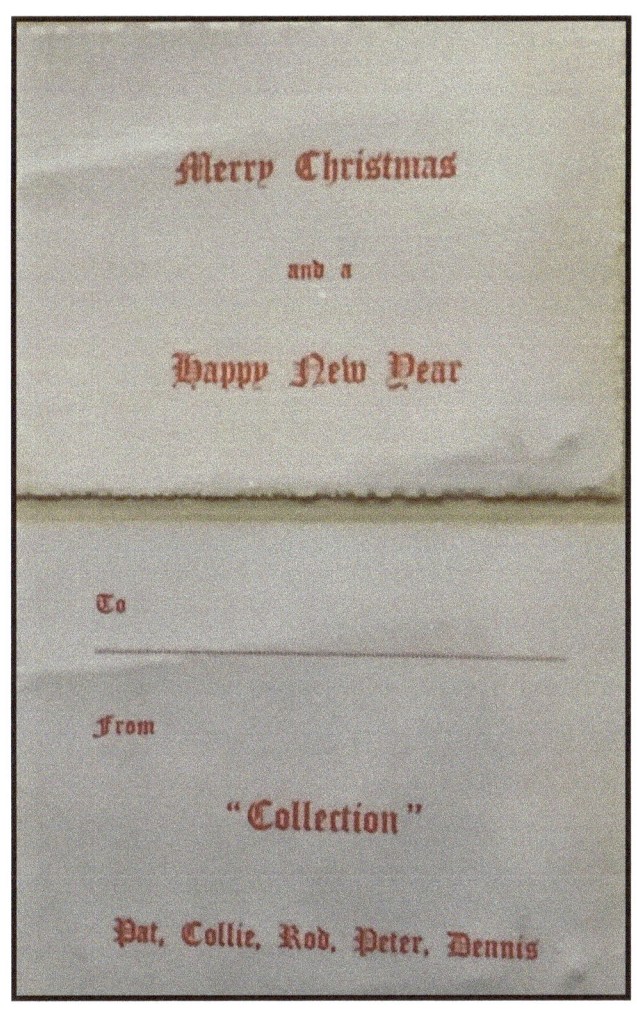

The 1968 or 1969 Collection Christmas Card – and who is "Collie"?

My memory is that Pat brought along a Christmas Card he had printed to send to our fans and supporters – it lists all the band members but the confusing thing is that one band member is referred to as "Collie" – is this "Collie" Moore or "Collie" Moses? I do not recall us ever referring to Unc as "Collie", but Porky reckons he often did. Seymour was called "Collie" at times although I think more so by the blokes in the footy team. Consequently, my thoughts were originally that the Christmas Card related to the 1969 Collection and the airport hangar gig, but it could be that it might have been produced for the newly named 1968 Collection, just prior to Seymour leaving the band! We'll never know! As well, Woody is referred to as "Rod" – as far as I can remember the only time we may have used Woody's real name, Rod[erick] was the day he was introduced to the rest of us back in early 1966 – after that, it was always Woody! I don't recall if any cards got sent but it would appear Pat had a few printed.

Popularity Shifts

In the band's first year in 1966, The Mystics played most of their gigs at The Rock and towns basically to the west and south-west - Lockhart, Collingullie, Yerong Creek, Culcairn and Walla Walla notwithstanding that of The Mystics first four paid gigs, three were in Wagga.

In 1967, The Mystics played 17 gigs at Wagga venues indicating that the band was getting a following in the city whilst continuing to play regularly at the same towns as in its first year. The Wagga gigs show the choice the punters had in terms of dance venues. Considering that, and despite the gigs played at the After 5 Club, the band was not yet on Wagga's prominent dance promoter's list for dances at Kyeamba Smith Hall, which was the big dance venue.

1968 started out well with the Subway/Noah's residency but following the fire in April, the lack of any gig diary being available impacted on identifiable gigs. Notwithstanding, the band still did 16 gigs in Wagga whilst the rest were scattered right across regular places but now included Batlow, Tumut, Temora and Coolamon. Interestingly, no identified gigs were found for Lockhart in 1968 despite The Mystics previous year's popularity in the town. The band also did gigs in Tumbarumba and had started to gain support in the town, notwithstanding the name change late in the year.

The shift in The Mystic's base from The Rock to Wagga started with the Subway/Noah's residency - gig ads started to describe The Mystics as "Wagga's Top Band", "Wagga's most popular" and the like so part of The Rock connection had been severed by early 1968. Reference to the Gig Guide clearly shows that the band did most of its gigs at The Rock in the first two years and Collection did quite a few with the pub residency in early 1969. Collection and its connection with Wagga became total in 1969 with the band playing 27 gigs in Wagga, 9 of which were at Kyeamba Smith Hall, Wagga's premier dance venue. As well, the band's gig focus was now on towns to the north, east and south-east of Wagga such as Junee, Tumut, Tumbarumba, Book Book, Coolamon, Ganmain and Batlow, as well as Griffith.

The Very Last Gig

In December, the band played two advertised gigs - Wesley Cabaret Room and The Rock Hall for the traditional Christmas Eve dance although Collection's gig schedule up to this point indicates that there would have been other gigs in the month. The Rock gig ad announced the last appearance of Collection at the hall where The Mystics played more gigs than any other venue since the band started. What the ad was referring to, was the last appearance of Collection "…with anyone from The Rock" in the band.

Again, Porky turned up sober! Neither Porky nor I can remember this last night despite it being, once again, a milestone gig – this happened a lot throughout the 4 years of the bands – important gigs passed without any special fanfare, memory or even photographic evidence.

The final gig for the last two band originals from The Rock!

I originally thought that we both played one more New Year's Eve gig but was given a photo of Porky which appeared in the Daily Advertiser dressed up as a Red Indian [see Odds and Sods] for a fancy dress 1969 New Year's Eve party somewhere consequently, he wasn't playing on NYE, therefore I wouldn't have been either!

So, Christmas Eve at The Rock Hall, 1969, was the final night for the remaining members of the band that came from The Rock and who were in the band at the start in 1965. It had been a ball. We started from scratch and basically taught ourselves how to play our instruments, we became a band, the band did more and more gigs each year and gained popularity, we made some money [but spent it] and the band was eventually voted the best band in Wagga. Most of all, we had fun throughout every stage the band went through!

Band Change

Both Porky and I had decided we would leave the band. I think girlfriends were becoming more important and they were becoming unhappy with sitting at home on weekends, and/or we were unhappy with them going out and becoming a target for other blokes, so we both finished up. We were replaced by Eric Rodgers on drums and Peter Nicol from The Final Four/The Dream, who had returned to Wagga, which left Woody as the only original member still playing in the band that we started in late 1965 - he wasn't in the very first band but as that band only went for a month or two with Des Condon, he is as good as being an original.

Neither Porky nor I can recall what our feelings were as a result of us no longer being in the band. Porky had had a short stint away from The Mystics after the 1968 fire, but I had been in the band continuously since the start. I guess our girlfriends soaked up the time now that we had weekends free! Notwithstanding that we both had had a great time playing since we started, not being able to go out with the girls and also, during the footy season missing out on after match socialising with our teammates, was something we now felt we wanted more than being in a band!

Gigs

The heaviest month was May with 10 gigs – two gigs every weekend for 5 weeks. November and June with 9 gigs each month – twice in June playing Friday, Saturday and Sunday gigs. There were 8 gigs in August and 7 in September and 6 in December. Reference to the Gig Guide shows that the band was working heavily right throughout the year and weekends with two and three gigs were common. Again, there are unidentified gigs which would have been played as a couple of months were rather lean compared to the more heavily booked months and considering the band being voted the most popular band in Wagga would have meant that it was in demand. Collection played 28 gigs in Wagga during the year signifying its popularity in the city and confirming that it was now a popular Wagga-based band. More gigs were played by Collection in 1969 than in any other year since the start in 1965.

A final observation

One thing that I noticed whilst compiling this story was how the band lined up on stage. Seymour always stood on Woody's inside with Les, and I was on the opposite end to Woody. When Pat joined, he stood right or left of Seymour and/or Unc, with Woody and I alternating our positions, on the opposite side to Pat. Woody and I changing positions did not make any difference to the overall sound although I have always thought that the bass player should be reasonably central on the stage so that the bass end, coupled with the drums, provides the bottom end link and back beat between all the other instruments rather than these coming from one side of the stage.

But the band played on!

The new Collection, [referred to as Collection 2 by the original members of Collection] continued with new members and became an even better band and won the Wagga section of Hoadley's National Battle of the Sounds in 1970 but unfortunately was beaten by a Newcastle band in the NSW Country Final in Sydney. The band subsequently broke up at the end of 1970 and Woody and Unc formed Oktoba with a new bass player and Eric Rogers on drums, which entered and won both the 1971 Wagga Battle of the Sounds and also the Victorian Country Final [for reasons unknown as they were a NSW band] and ended up in the Grand Final at Festival Hall, Melbourne - a mighty effort! Of course, they didn't win because the final contained popular top recording bands at the time. In 1972 they again won the Wagga Battle of the Sounds but were beaten in Sydney in the NSW Country section. The band split up towards the end of 1972.

When I returned in September 1972 after more than two years working in Papua New Guinea, Woody asked me to join him and Eric Rogers, as a three-piece Oktoba [which is referred to as Oktoba 2 by the original members of Oktoba]. This band played some great gigs, especially one supporting a terrific New Zealand band called The Cleves, at Kyeamba Smith Hall. Oktoba 2 was very tight, played quite a few gigs at the John Macarther Hotel, which became a popular night spot, but lasted only about 6 - 8 months before the band broke up when I got married in June 1973.

After leaving Oktoba, Unc had joined The Townsmen who had a residency at the Wagga RSL Club until he was unceremoniously sacked one night by the club manager for sneaking a quick drink on stage during a lull in the stage act. Following this, Unc then formed Opus with three other musos which went for a couple of years.

Woody and Pat formed a band called Kasino [which included Nick Freeman on drums, previously mentioned and who comes into the story with the 2007 Reunion Concert] and which went for about 3 years before breaking up and Woody subsequently moving to Sydney to pursue a full-time musical career.

After I got married, I joined a popular local country band called Mayberry Park on a temporary basis for about 4 months and then accepted an offer to join the Riverina Jazz Band on a permanent basis, in late 1973. After nearly 5 years, I left that band to form Duke with Pat which lasted from 1978 – 1982 and which also included Nick Freeman. When Duke folded, the last connection back to the original band from The Rock and its various people who had played in both The Mystics and Collection, ended - but the mateships have remained.

The best years!

There is no doubt that The Mystics and Collection were playing in the most vibrant period for bands – from the mid-1960s until the end of the decade. Apart from the number of venues operating in Wagga, dances in small towns in the region always attracted crowds irrespective of where the town or hall was situated – a prime example was The Mystics New Year's Eve 1966 dance at Pleasant Hills – the place only had a hall, a pub and primary school yet it drew a huge crowd in the middle of nowhere. Likewise, the Myall Park and Mullengandra B&S balls were held in halls which were the only structures for miles around. The regularity of dances at The Rock, especially in the first two years, did not diminish attendances and they were always well supported, not only by the locals but from Wagga and other near towns. Lockhart and Henty dances generally relied on local support, but the numbers were always worth playing to. The same could be said for Tumbarumba, Tumut, Batlow and Junee but Kyeamba Smith Hall was always a favoured big gig venue – on occasions, The Mystics and Collection played to over 1000 kids!

Reference to the Gig Towns map shows that the bands played in or at 28 towns or isolated gig venues – this includes venues where The Mystics played woolshed dances for The Rock Yerong Creek footy club. I doubt too many other bands around at the time would have covered the district as much as The Mystics and or Collection and this was because we were originally a band that came from a small town and our early gigs were playing in small towns. I cannot recall any other small town in the general area that had a band and as mentioned elsewhere in this story, The Mystics especially, and to a certain extent, Collection, had fan bases in other towns e.g. Henty, Lockhart, Tumbarumba whilst Collection's fan base was principally Wagga.

Whilst the early 1970s continued as a good period for local bands, the scene started to change from the early to mid-1970s. Dance venues started to close and there was a shift away from the small town hall dance venues of the 1960s and into the club scene. I have always believed this was largely due to the big clubs offering a Saturday night out with a large auditorium filled with people who had to book weeks ahead to get in, a band, supper which was usually a choice of chicken in a basket or nothing, and availability of alcohol at the bar rather than outside out of the boot of a car.

The mass interest in, and popularity of, music which exploded when The Beatles and other legendary bands emerged, created the scene for The Mystics and Collection in the latter part of the 1960s – I doubt the music scene will ever again create the impact and influence on bands that we saw and were part of. The Mystics and Collection's experiences would have been very similar to thousands of bands formed in country areas and towns. Very few ever got the chance, or even wanted to try the big scene in Melbourne or Sydney. At times I think we did discuss whether we should have a crack but in the end, we were all working day jobs and were often doubling our normal weekly pay with weekend band income [tax free], so the lure of a chance at any fame was not all that attractive against the money we were making. This was the reason that Pat decided not to go to Melbourne with The End, and I think he convinced us we were far better off staying local – let's be the big fish in a small pond syndrome! The End/Final Four did take the step and as good as they were, they found it tough going to break into the big time, although The Dream, with Jack McGrath, and Terry Stirzaker, for a shorter time, did have an impact but whether this transferred into making any money, is doubtful.

I have, over the years, read many biographies of well-known bands from the 1960s and it's interesting to note that there were a lot of parallels between what happened to these groups during their early years and climb to fame, and what happened to The Mystics and Collection in their journey over 4 years to be voted Wagga's best band. The highlights [plenty] and the lows [fortunately not many], the fun bits, the mateship, the places we played at and the people we met and who became fans all add up to great memories, and as the punters showed with the Reunion concerts, they too have never forgotten those great days. Despite a general lack of photographs, I managed to find enough together with paper articles and gig ads, to turn a few memories into a reasonably accurate chronologically documented written story.

We saw the best time in music and were a part of it, and that's why the four years I was in The Mystics and Collection are a very special period in my life. The success of The Mystics, which was widely known as "The band from The Rock", is part of The Rock's history and as such, should be acknowledged. This was one of the main reasons I have written this story – to have some recognition of the band's achievements and popularity recorded in the museum at The Rock – as Verdo said, "The Mystics put The Rock on the map!" The continuation, under the new name, Collection, which contained three of the original members from The Rock and Yerong Creek, deserves to be included in that recognition.

Not the Final Chapter

Take a Mystical step back in time

If you loved the 60s then mark Saturday, April 30 in your diary. For one night only, two of the Riverina's most popular bands are joining together in a one-off performance at Kyeamba Smith Hall.

Catch The Mystics and Collection in their 40-year anniversary reunion as they play their versatile covers from the 60s, including hits from The Beatles, The Hollies, The Kinks, Cream, Creedence, The Stones, The Animals, Deep Purple and Led Zeppelin.

Compere for the evening will be 2WG's Peter Alibon and tickets for this special event are on sale now.

The original band, The Mystics, formed in 1965 with boys from The Rock and Yerong Creek, but then changed their name to Collection after a couple of changes in their line-up.

The band was extremely popular in the Riverina and played regularly to capacity crowds around the area. They also played as the back-up band for Ronnie Burns in Wagga in 1968 and were voted best Riverina Band at the time.

Tickets for this reunion concert are $20 per person and can be purchased from Allison Music, Don Tuckwell Audio, Peter L Brown & Associates, The Rock Supermarket and The Rock Post Office.

Bookings will also be taken for tables of 10 but must be pre-paid. A bar will operate during the night and food and other beverages will also be available to purchase during the evening.

All proceeds from this event will be donated to The Rock and District Aged Care Facility Committee.

For more information, contact Ann McCole on 6920 1023.

One of the Daily Advertiser articles on the bands and the Reunion Concert

In 2004 I was approached by a member of a fund-raising committee, who were raising money to build an aged care facility at The Rock, with a request to consider getting the band back together again as a fund raiser. For some time I had been thinking, just for fun, that it would be great to get back together simply for jam sessions, playing songs that we did back in the 60s and to hopefully revisit the great feelings and mateship we had had during the four years that both bands were going. The fund-raising request gave me the reason and provided the impetus.

I contacted all the principal band members and surprisingly, everyone readily agreed. There would be challenges as Porky and Les had virtually stopped playing when they left the band nearly 40 years ago. Seymour had continued to sing at weddings, in church, at funerals and social events using midi files compiled by Pat, but in a very much laid-back style and certainly not the pop and rock songs that would be needed for the reunion. Pat, Unc and I were all still involved in the local music scene which meant that we still had playing chops. Woody had moved to Sydney and taken his musical career much further than the rest of us and was a special challenge because of the distance and his involvement with the very well-known and popular group, The Delltones. They were doing a lot of work for 6 months of the year as well as corporate gigs at times in the off-season - Woody was also working with a small band on the side. The Delltones were very reluctant to give Woody any special leave to attend rehearsals [but they did], or the concert night itself, and it wasn't until very late that they eventually agreed to him having the reunion weekend off so he could do the gig.

All band members turned up for the original meeting to map out the year, at which it was decided that 12 months would be needed to get both bands up to a standard that would be acceptable, not only to the punters, but more importantly, to the band members themselves. Rehearsals were commenced in about April/May 2004, often without Woody although he was kept up to date with what songs we were learning and a couple of times during the year, he came down from Sydney for a weekend of solid rehearsals. The rehearsals were initially a fair bit of hard work for band members playing again for the first time in 40 years, but they were mostly also a lot of fun.

Dave Wall – Keyboards

At the original meeting, it was suggested by Woody that we engage a keyboard player as a lot of the songs both bands would be doing included keyboards. Whilst we never had keyboards back in the 60s, it was agreed that this would be a great addition to the overall sound. There was one unanimous choice, Dave Wall, a highly regarded Wagga keyboards player who had been around the music scene for many years. Dave accepted the offer and not only provided keyboards, but also terrific keyboard brass backing in songs where brass was a prominent feature. He assisted with chord charts and his input throughout the year was valued by both bands. Dave was also invited back for the 2007 reunion concert.

Dave Wall – keyboards - a unanimous choice!

A lot of discussion was had in respect to which songs each band would do. They needed to be from the years of the two bands - songs were generally kept to the original versions with each band rehearsing on separate nights generally, at least once a week. Peter Alibon, [ex-Lost and Found and Captain Walker bass player], an announcer at 2WG, came on side and he did a great job throughout the year giving us free advertising on his breakfast show by frequently ringing Woody or me for an early morning update on progress of rehearsals. Conversely, Les Pridmore, the lead singer with Lost and Found/Captain Walker, and who was at the time of the reunion, a high profile Sydney radio announcer and "shock jock" going under the name of George Moore and sometime replacement for John Laws, was contacted with the intention that the reunion of The Mystics and Collection would receive some high profile support from him as he was in the other good band in Wagga at that time and would have remembered The Mystics. His band was regarded as Wagga's Rolling Stones and The Mystics were regarded as Wagga's Beatles. Rather snobbishly, when contacted, he denied any memory of Wagga or The Mystics, so the expected radio exposure died in the arse! Thanks, Les - we remember you, though! Jock McKenzie also told me a story about someone going to Sydney after Pridmore had moved there and got a job with 2SM. The person called in at the radio station hopefully to catch up with him after he finished his session. When the message was passed to Pridmore he simply sent a message back to the reception desk saying he did not remember Wagga or anyone from there. Interestingly, Wikipedia lists him as being born in Wagga, playing in Lost and Found and originally working for 2WG! Good one, Les!

The Daily Advertiser gave the band excellent coverage over the 12 months of organisation and rehearsals and we had articles and photos in the paper during the year on a number of occasions As well, the Riverina Conservatorium of Music in Wagga, kindly allowed us to occasionally use a rehearsal room at their campus.

The reunion concert took place on the 30th April 2005, almost 40 years after the band first started. The concert/dance/reunion was held at Kyeamba Smith Hall, the favoured big gig venue for both bands from past days. The committee did a fantastic job decorating the hall with blown-up photos of The Mystics around the walls as well as a lot of other decoration. Two 1960s Mini Minors with racing stripes, one either side of the stage, added a special nostalgic touch – a real blow-back to the era! When we arrived at Kyeamba Smith Hall on the night, there was a long line people waiting to get in - Porky thought that they were there for the motor bike races that were also on at the showground that night and the noise of which we had to contend with at times, throughout the night. We were staggered when nearly over 850 punters turned up with reports that people had travelled from Perth, Brisbane, Melbourne Tasmania and Sydney as well as many other places around the state and district. There were large buses parked in the hall carpark indicating large groups had come in from towns around the district - even Des Condon turned up - we had not seen him since the late 1960s! My old bass teacher, Terry Stirzaker also came, due to his special friendship with Pat.

The standing around and waiting to go on stage had everyone on edge and this was exacerbated by the knowledge that the crowd was huge. The committee hired white coats for The Mystics, and I had a black Reunion T-shirt commemorating the night made for each band member of The Mystics and Collection – the black and white being an acknowledgement back to The Rock Yerong Creek footy team colours. Finally, we were individually announced onto the stage and kicked into the opening number, "Sgt Pepper", with Unc on vocals having re-written the words to include all the names of the band members into the lyrics. As per the album, this segued into "With little help from my friends" with Seymour taking over lead vocals. Any early concerns evaporated as we gradually worked through the first set, which went very well – Seymour handling Mystics vocals for the first half of each set which included both Les and Pat, with Unc coming on to complete the second half of the set with Pat, Woody, Porky and me as Collection The feeling behind the stage after the first set was simply relieved euphoria – and Peter Alibon drank most of our beer!

Les had problems with a finger on his left hand, the hand used for forming the chords. The middle finger wouldn't bend enough for him to be able to form a major bar chord – an old football injury. He eventually solved the problem by bending and taping the offending finger permanently into the required position – can't remember what he did when a minor, augmented or diminished chord came up in a song! We probably still got a major chord!

The night was a success both for the committee and most of all, both bands. The Mystics and Collection managed to get through a total of about 60+ songs or so from the 1960's and it was an achievement for Porky, Les and Seymour that they were able to contribute after so many years of not being in a band. On the other hand, Pat, Woody, Unc and myself, were able to keep the band together and sounding good all night, and Dave Wall's keyboard contribution added loads to the sound. Yeah, we made some blues, but in the end, the punters loved us! Woody said that, notwithstanding all the gigs he had done all over Australia with The Delltones, and all the other bands he had played with since the early years both in Wagga and Sydney, he was more nervous leading up to the first set than he had been for any other gig

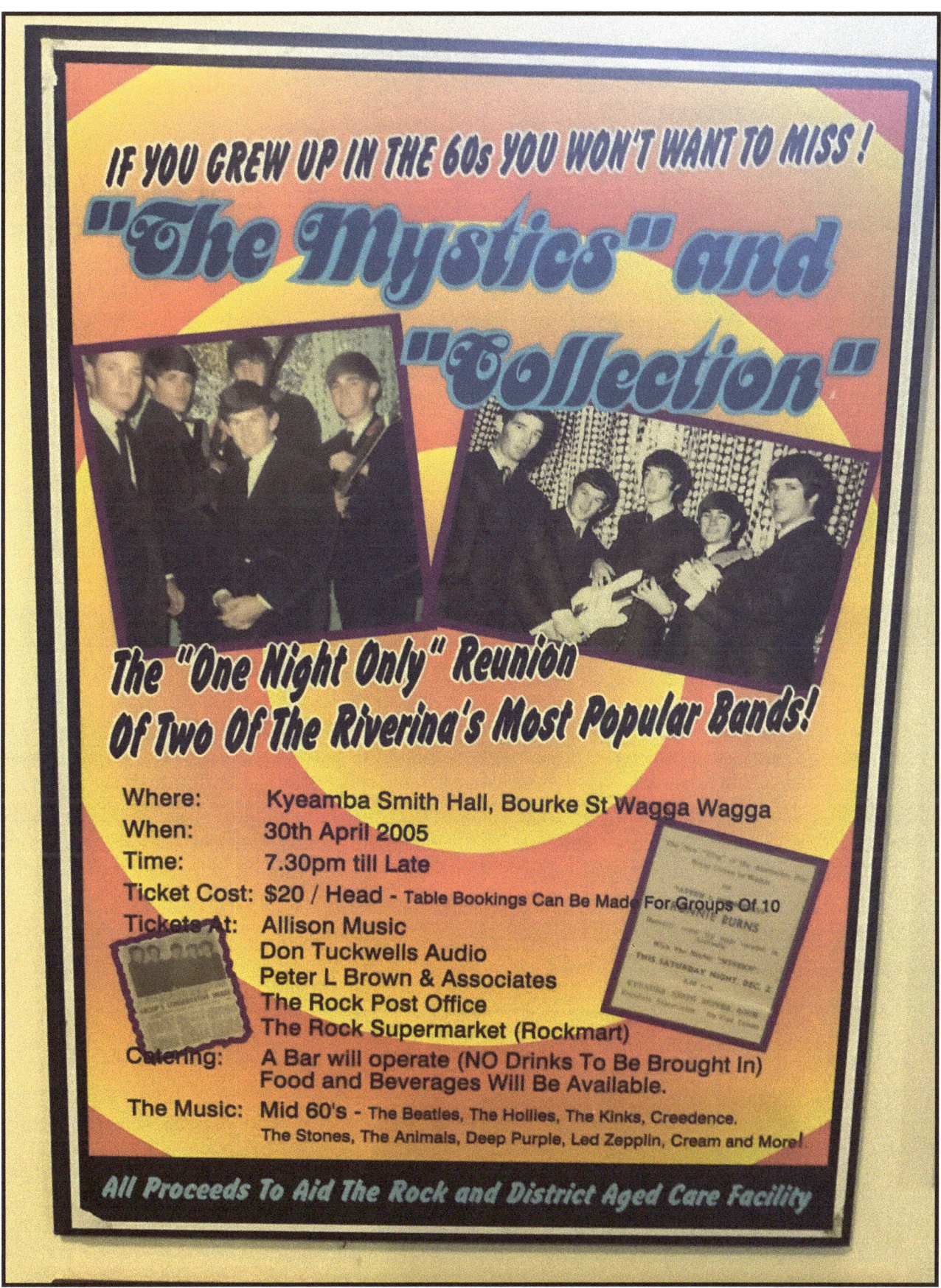

Reunion 2005 Poster – it really worked as a crowd puller

The opening number 2005 Reunion Concert, Kyeamba Smith Hall

in his musical career, and the reunion meant more to him than any other musical event he had been involved in or with! The same goes for me! We roared through the night to the huge crowd's approval with people jammed up against the stage, either dancing or simply watching the band or taking photos or videos. The night was recorded on a mobile 24 track recording machine as well as at the audio desk by Wayne Sims, our audio man who had spent most of the day building the sound system – he did a fantastic job. Simsy was impressed – he said he wasn't even born when the bands were going around but the size of the crowd showed how popular the bands must have been.

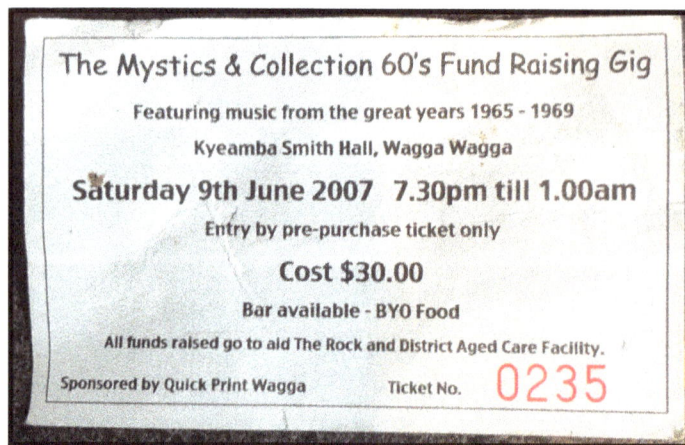

Over 800 tickets sold for the second reunion concert!

The concert was also videoed but not as successfully as hoped because filming a band needs independent cameras with cameramen to be able to focus on different people in the band. Notwithstanding, the video is still a memento of the night, warts and all. We just accept Woody doing a raging solo on the audio, but the camera is zoomed in on Les or Porky – or someone else!

The next day, the band members gathered at the Browns for a casual recovery lunch and de-brief – a bunch of very happy much older members of The Mystics and Collection, which all started at The Rock - and there was some emotion evident which might have been influenced by the amount of alcohol consumed!

The Reunion Concert was so successful, the committee requested we consider doing another fund raiser and this was done on the 9th July, 2007, to which about 800 punters turned up. Again, the night was a great success, but it was agreed by all members of both bands that the 2007 reunion concert was the final chapter for both The Mystics and Collection. I think about $20,000 was raised from the two concerts – and we couldn't even get the toilet block in the new aged care facility named after us, when it was built! The first concert had been an absolute buzz, and whilst the second concert was a lot of fun and even showcased better musicianship, trying to emulate the success a third time was simply not a goer. The T-shirts which were made commemorating the night, showed on the back a tongue-in-cheek "Australian Tour Dates" - with none listed

Front of T-shirt

Back of T-shirt

Nick Freeman – Drums

At the time rehearsals started for the 2007 reunion concert, Porky was being treated for a concerning medical condition and decided that he would not be able to handle a full night of drumming for both bands. It was decided to call in Nick Freeman, a good local drummer, who Unc, Woody, Pat and I had all played with in different bands after our Mystics and Collection days. Nick had been the drummer with the Tin Soldiers back in the late 1960's, who were reasonably popular at the time.

As Porky decided he would play drums only in The Mystics sets, Nick handled the Collection brackets. The night was videoed, this time with three cameras - two fixed and one mobile, and whilst it produced a better video than 2005, again, featured solos weren't always captured. The performance was also again recorded on a 24-track mobile recording machine, and the sound and playing was much improved over the 2005 concert, although there was the occasional stuff up such as me playing the first verse of "Itchykoo Park" in A, the original key, whilst the band played it in the rehearsed key of G! Thankfully, Unc managed to re-mix my bass parts from the rest of the song over the bad bits on the audio to turn an awful bass sound into the proper bass sound on the recording! After nearly 40 years of playing bass in bands, I can't believe it took me a whole verse to work out that the crap sound I was producing was due to me being in the wrong key.

It was great to have both Dave Wall and Nick Freeman involved in the 2007 reunion. They added to the overall sound and contributed greatly on the night. Again, Simsy did the audio for the second concert – a real professional and his expertise gave the bands a great sound.

Nick Freeman - stand-in drummer for Collection in 2007

The day after – and why I bothered!

The day after the 2005 Reunion Concert – very relieved, happy and relaxed!
L to R: Seymour, Pat, Brownie, Woody, Porky, Unc and Les

The photo above says it all! This is not just a photo of a group of happy musos having a drink on a Sunday afternoon – it's a photo of a group of happy musos having a drink on a Sunday afternoon in 2005, who played in a couple of bands 40+ years ago and stayed mates and who, the night before, had played at a great reunion concert which drew a huge crowd to see them as The Mystics and Collection on stage again. As many of the punters said during the night, it was also a reunion for them because it brought them back to Wagga for the night where they re-connected with friends and acquaintances for the first time in many years. It was rumoured that hardly a person could be found in The Rock the night of the reunion – the whole town was at the concert at the showgrounds in Wagga!

So, why have I taken the time to put these few years of my life into print? Initially, my intention was to put together a short history of the two bands which was to be available to the punters at the 2005 Reunion Concert, but I simply ran out of time, and it was never completed. The onset of, and lockdown caused by, the Corona virus in March 2020 was the impetus to finish the history, and it has been a very enjoyable time-eater when I couldn't do much else – and the exercise has taken on a life of its own!

The underlying reason was that I did something with some mates in which we all had a common purpose, gaining tremendous satisfaction from creating something from nothing and, then making that something better, notwithstanding a couple of personnel changes - and had a lot of fun. The secondary reason was that I believe The Mystics, principally, should be acknowledged in The Rock Museum as part of The Rock's history – history isn't all about what happened a hundred years or more ago!

To be in a band which was part of a musical explosion and musical change that represents the best period of music development of our lifetime, was an opportunity we all grabbed. The Shadows started it for us, the British invasion bands, especially The Beatles, made it exciting and the development that took place during the 1960s influenced how bands played and with the newer styles of beat, blues, pop and rock music, enticed us into wanting to be part of what was happening. The formation, popularity and success of The Mystics was something unique to The Rock and should be recognised as part of The Rock's history, and the extension of the original band by Collection's achievements and popularity, round off the overall story of A Band from The Rock.

Researching local papers and coming across an ad for The Mystics or Collection after 50 years was very satisfying and, at times, caused some emotion because the number of ads I found made me realise how popular the bands were and how often they played gigs. Whilst a limited number of gigs and events still linger in memories for different reasons [although sometimes the factual content has been warped by faded memories], as I have found in researching the gigs, locating photos and paper articles about both bands, there was a hell of a lot none of us remember and milestone dates or gigs were virtually never recorded photographically. Little snippets, however, did emerge out of the fog the more I pressed the band members to try and recall anything from those days. Apart from Pat who had photos taken, and Woody who kept most of his diaries, the rest of us, nor our immediate families, did nothing to preserve these few fantastic years for posterity. Despite the achievement of forming a band and getting it to a point where it became popular, whilst satisfying at the time, did not seem to occur to us that it held any special significance as far as we were concerned. Although most of us have kept some memorabilia, when asking for items I found we all kept almost the same stuff. Virtually every special milestone was simply part of being in the band and treated as a part of our daily lives at the time, just as playing footy for The Rock-Yerong Creek was part of our sporting life, and we didn't keep too much about our footy efforts either. The need to remember all the good bits was not recognised then and the importance of all those milestones only becomes important now, and it's too late! Notwithstanding this, I hope with the foregoing, I have managed to re-create our "band" days!

The Gig Guide at the end of this story shows how often The Mystics and Collection cumulatively played at The Rock [over 60 gigs], and this was mirrored in other towns that I visited in search of local paper's gig ads – the local band was very popular in its home town [not surprisingly]. The Impacts did most of the gigs in Tumut, as well as Talbingo and Batlow, The Shades likewise in Young, The Wimowehs in Temora and the Lost and Found/Captain Walker did most of the gigs at The After 5 and Kyeamba Smith Hall after The End left in 1967 and up until they themselves left Wagga in late 1968. The Mystics and Collection were undisputedly the popular band at The Rock but also at St. Joseph's in Wagga, and eventually, in the second half of 1969, at Kyeamba Smith Hall. I believe from what I have located, The Mystics and Collection were the next most popular band in Tumut to The Impacts and both The Mystics and Collection were also very popular in Lockhart, Henty and Tumbarumba, towns which did not have a local band. Both bands did over 60 identified gigs at Wagga dance venues over the 4 years and from my research, this was much more than any other

Wagga-based band. To a lesser extent, Collection was popular in Junee for a brief period in 1969. A major factor was that The Mystics and Collection were basically one band and went for 4 years – most of the other Wagga bands around at the same time never achieved this longevity and generally broke up after a quick burst across the local music scene.

As already mentioned, one area I didn't find an ad for either band was for B&S - type balls and dances, yet both The Mystics and Collection played these types of gigs - Myall Park B&S, Wagga B&S, Coolamon B&S and Holbrook B&S, Wagga Country Club, and downstairs at the Wagga RSL Club, and their recoveries the next night. The reason these were not advertised was they were invitation only, aimed at the upper levels of local society and out of town "blue bloods"!

The Wrap Up!

Musically, the times were exciting, and we were a part of it all! For four young mates from The Rock, who were team-mates in the local footy side and who had grown up together, the band was an exciting adventure. For one young lad from Yerong Creek, joining The Mystics gave him the opportunity to use his musical ability when opportunities in Yerong Creek were non-existent whilst at the same time, allowing him to join in a very strong mateship with four other like-minded budding musicians! In fact, being part of a successful band was like being part of a successful premiership footy side – group success and achievement is the foundation of lifelong group connection and mateship!

When the band started, we couldn't play a note but within a very short space of time, the band was playing paid gigs and the more gigs we played, the better we became. The better we became, the more gigs we got, and the local fans loved and followed us as did fan bases in other towns. Over the 4 years, we went from starting at The Rock and being very inexperienced, to being voted the best band in Wagga, appreciating that there were a couple of band changes.

Les started things off when he bought his first guitar, and the rest of us followed. Porky bought a guitar as well but then changed to drums - and I got a bass. Seymour was recruited and Des added to our early very limited musical knowledge and ability and when Woody joined the band, things started to improve. When Pat initially joined on a temporary basis, he not only became the source of the songs we played but he also brought a professional musicality to the band because of his experience and knowledge, and when he decided he liked the band and wanted to be a permanent member, it was an opportunity that the band could not pass up, despite meaning Les would have to leave!

With Seymour leaving just before, and Porky just after, the Noah's fire, the next few months when Jock and Dick joined were still fun and the band remained popular. However, coming from a small town where the original members grew up together proved to be too strong a connection and consequently, Seymour and Porky returned to The Mystics. Notwithstanding best of intentions, the pressure of farm work finally brought Seymour's membership of the group to an end within a couple of months of the band reuniting! When Unc joined, the band was able to continue the upward improvement and progression and the vocals and harmonies became stronger, and the band got tighter - and it was still great fun despite two original members no longer being involved. Both new members fitted in and the band got better and better.

There are only a couple of negatives as I see it –
a] that we had to ask Les to leave the band so Pat could join;
b] the severe lack of photos of the original band;
c] that we did not see the importance of keeping more info and memorabilia from that time.

After more than 50 years of me being involved in bands and music generally, playing pop, rock, country and jazz [and for a short period, even old time], being involved in musical theatre, doing classic band shows, completing a 10 year stint in the Albury Carols by Candlelight Band backing numerous national and local artists, recording a few albums with other local musicians, the very best years of my involvement in music for fun and musical excitement were the first years. Since the early years, I have played in bands with very competent and experienced musicians and whilst the musical side was satisfying, the fun was never the same as it was playing with mates who all started out together – it was simply a very special period in my life – and the band came from The Rock!

Peter Brown

18th October 2020

Photos

The one colour photo of The Mystics from 1966 was taken either by one of Seymour's sisters or an unidentified relative. The very bulk of the rest of the photos of the band were taken with Pat's camera by fans consequently these are from November 1967 after Woody completed his exams and returned to the band and Les left. The early photos of Les and me with our guitars are evidence that the Magrath family had a camera, but it seems it never made it to a gig – bummer! No-one else in the band had a camera and surprisingly, none of our parents, who were involved in running the dances at The Rock, thought to take any photos even if they had one [my mother had a box brownie camera – again, bummer]. I also contacted a few former female fans to see if they had any photos in old albums, but the common response was none owned a camera in those days. There must be photos out there somewhere, unfortunately most likely yellowing in old photo albums!

The photos of Collection were principally Daily Advertiser photos, as well as some taken by Eric Rogers, some by fans with Pat's camera and a couple that remain unknown as to their source. I am sure there are others out there somewhere as well, but discovery would be a long shot.

Had we had mobile phones in those days, there would have been thousands to pick from.

Postscripts

As I sit here finishing off this story on the 18th October, 2020, about a group of young blokes who played music together in The Mystics and Collection, I realise that I have left out one important piece of information relative to these band years.

Postscript 1 – The girlfriends

Of the seven principal members of the two bands, all bar one married their girlfriends from those band days, and remain married to those same girls – Pat was the only dissenter, marrying someone not associated with this story or time period and, unfortunately, it did not last although I believe that it was a reasonably amicable split. The fact that a band of musos have remained married to their original choice of a life's partner is a major departure from the reputation that musicians generally have with respect to matrimonial longevity and bliss!

****

This morning, the 19th October 2020, I was going over and reviewing all that I had written because yesterday, I had basically finished the story. As I was sitting here in my music room checking spelling, typos and punctuation, my mobile rang – it was Woody in Sydney to tell me he had just had a call from Stan Wright [another local ex-bass player] to say that Pat had passed away overnight and suddenly, the importance of getting this story finished suffered a massive reality check in that Pat will never get to read the story nor realise what an important part of both band's successes he was. I know he would probably have challenged little bits here and there despite my regular contact with him over the past 6 months clarifying bits that needed clarifying or confirmation of a memory or recollection. I know he would have loved what I have written, not because of his influence but because he was genuinely proud to have been part of The Mystics and Collection years. I now need to add postscript 2.

****

Postscript 2 – Pat "Pattie" Geaghan

One additional point I had intended to make in this story is that up until yesterday I was able to say that we are all still on the planet, some 50 years after the bands ended. This statistic is quite unusual because of the length of time that has passed since our band days, and notwithstanding that it is very pleasing for each of us, a number have had close calls with health, medical and accident issues. However, it had slipped out of my mind until I got the phone call that, very sadly and suddenly, Pat left us sometime in the early hours of this morning, the 19th October 2020, for that big gig in the sky and apart from "breaking up the band[s] forever", that ends the chance of one more reunion, whether we wanted to or not! "Pattie", as I always called him, will be a huge loss to all of us – he was Mr Music – he knew the chords, he knew the words and who wrote them, he knew how many versions of the song had been recorded [and he probably had a copy of each], and he could play the song using four different inversions of each chord in the song.

Pat was a font of musical knowledge, a cool and calming influence, he was never angry, never judgmental, and never demanding, and totally unselfish. He never pushed himself to the front but was a steadying influence from the rear, totally reliable and always ready to help and/or provide advice [particularly on all things musical], he was a pacifist who accepted his lot in life with the motto - "what it is, is what it is!" Despite the health and sight difficulties he had experienced over the past 10 years or more, he remained totally upbeat [a great descriptive" musical" word for Pattie's approach to life generally]. When his health deteriorated with a diabetic condition which placed him on the kidney transplant list, he was quite prepared to miss out because he felt younger suffers of the same condition would be more deserving. For simply having that attitude, he deserved to get a new one, and thankfully he did!

I spoke with Pattie on the phone last Friday and he told me that he had been diagnosed with cancer but it appeared to have not spread – I am sure he lied to me deliberately because we now know that he was seriously ill and I believe he did not want me to be concerned – that is typical of Pattie, thinking of others before himself. On Saturday and Sunday, I left voicemail messages on his phone but got no response. Again, I originally believed he was shielding me from the real situation he was facing consequently, and when I got the call on Monday that he had left us, I was emotionally wounded, and still can't accept that he is gone! I have since been advised that he had lost his voice in the last couple of days so he wouldn't have been able to talk, even if he wanted to.

Throughout the writing of The Mystics and Collection story, I phoned Pattie frequently with the words "I need to pick your brain"! It would be about something that occurred during the band years or a gig we played, and his memory was pretty good. I am so glad that I reached the end of the story last Sunday because it would be very difficult to accept that I have lost not only a long and valued friend, but also, a great source of past band information.

Pattie's approach to life was very simple – it was not cluttered with things negative in any aspect, and it was always thus! If we all had Pattie's outlook on life and relationships, the world would be a much, much better place.

All the members of The Mystics and Collection have some part of their musical talents and experiences to thank Pattie for, and to acknowledge the influence that he was, and had, in our development as band members and as a band. We are all better because Pat joined the band that started at The Rock!

I just wish he hadn't thrown out his gig diaries from 1967- 69!

Peter Brown
19th October 2020

P.S. The above was delivered as part of the eulogy I gave at his funeral.

Some comments and quotes [unconfirmed]:

"The reason I spat the dummy in Wagga the night we played with The Mystics was because they were better than us – the shits!"
Russell Morris/Somebody's Image

****

"I will never forget The Mystics – what a great band but they put me under pressure one night at Noahs with a song that was too high for me and it took over a week for my gonads to drop back down".
Jon Blanchfield

****

"Despite our win, Collection were the best band by far at The Battle of the Sounds in 1969 – our band was shit but fortunately our drummer was banging one of the judges, so they never stood a chance!"
Nanna's Passion Pit

****

"The Mystics? Never heard of 'em!" Les Pridmore
"Les Pridmore? Never heard of him!" The Mystics

****

"How much did you f****** say? You can't be f****** serious – all that for only a couple of f****** hours? We've hardly taken anything at the f****** door! That's highway f****** robbery!"
The Priest at St. Josephs

****

"I'm getting some special shirts made for you boys to wear on stage". Kath Pill
[a] "That sounds great, Mrs Pill!" Collection
[b] "You must be joking! They're f****** awful! This is a pop and rock band not a
f****** Mardi Gras band! How do we get out of this residency! Collection

****

"Hello Mrs. Finlayson – is there any chance Woody could be here by tomorrow for today's practice?"
The Mystics

****

"It's got me buggered! This pops bucket sits inside the hall in the back-room and every time I come and get it to spread on the dance floor, it's as damp as buggery – and smells a bit funny!"
Pops spreader at The Rock Hall

****

"The bass sounds shithouse! It sounds out-of-tune! Brownie
"Try moving your fingers down two frets!" Pat

****

"Oops – too late! You should have said something sooner".
One of the Band

****

"Guess what, fellas! I think that last speaker has just started to play up".
Les

****

"Welcome to the band, Jock! You can put all your gear in the Noahs storeroom with ours – it'll be totally safe in there!"
The Mystics

****

"Now for our second bracket, we'd like to play the same 5 songs we did in the first bracket"
The Mystics – very first gig

****

"Now for our third bracket, we'd like to play the same 5 songs we did in the second bracket – but in a different order"

The Mystics – same gig

The Mystics 1966

Collection 1969

The Mystics - 2005 Reunion Concert, Kyeamba Smith Hall

Collection - 2005 Reunion Concert, Kyeamba Smith Hall

The Mystics and Collection – opening number 2007 Reunion Concert

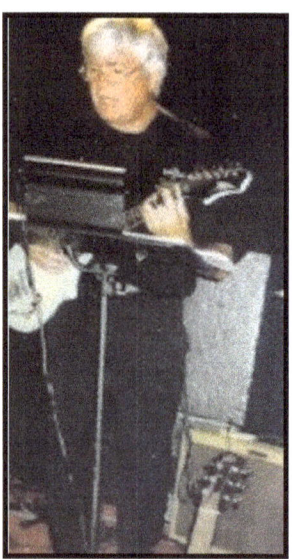  

The song list from the first Reunion Concert – 30th April 2005

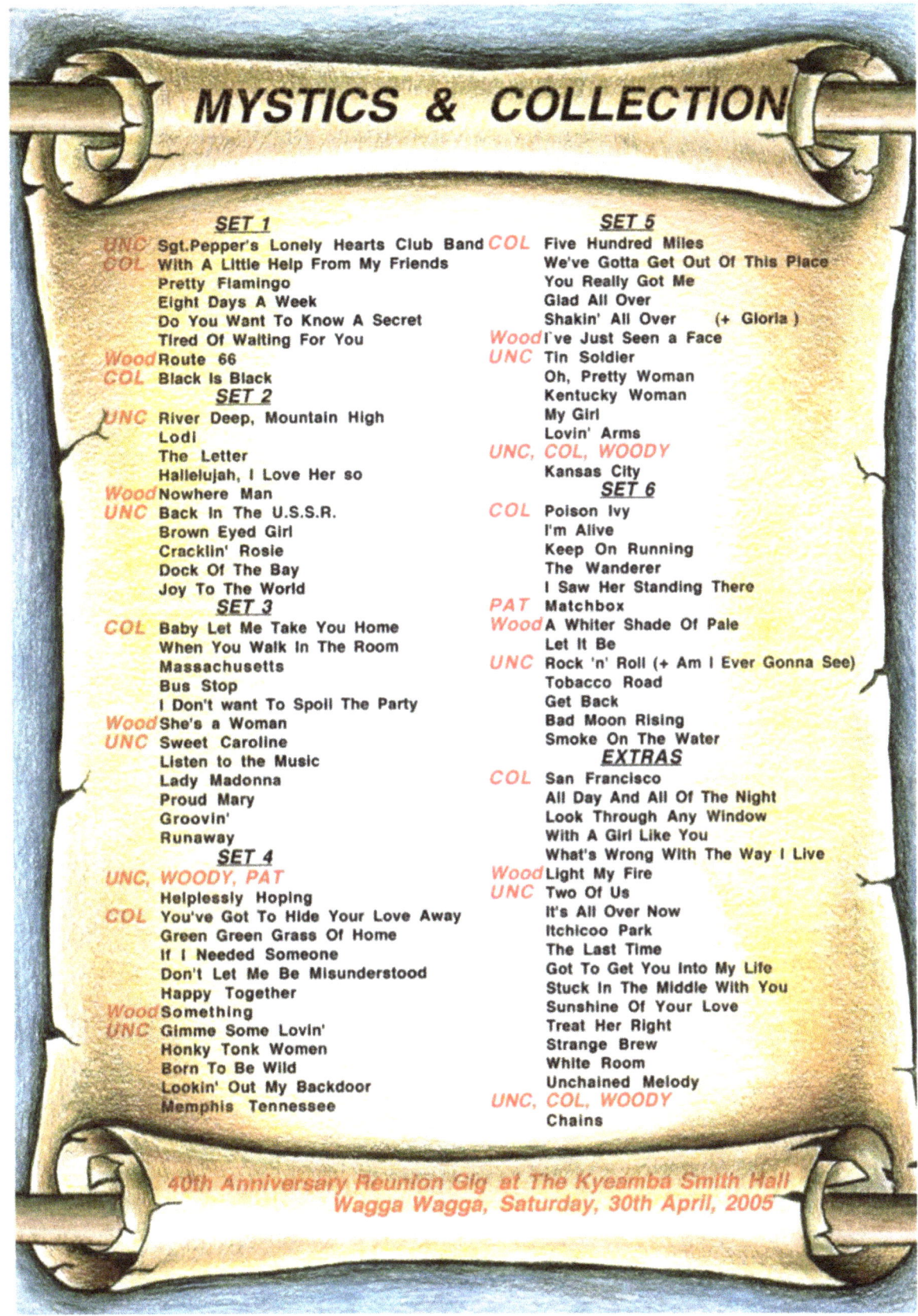

One song which was never on our song lists from the band years –
The Angels – "Am I ever going to see your face again" – but for crowd reaction,
it had to be included!

Gig Towns, Venues and Dates

The great majority of the following dates largely relate to identified gigs from either newspaper ads or articles in The Daily Advertiser, The Tumut and Adelong Times, Tumbarumba Times, Area News and associated publications, The Temora Independent, The Eastern Riverina Chronicle [Henty] and the Junee Southern Cross.

The Lockhart Review and Urana Advertiser was limited to 1966 and 1969 editions only. Woody's diaries, although incomplete over the 4 years, filled in a lot of the gaps where paper advertising was not found or simply did not occur. The below map shows the towns, and out of town venues, where The Mystics and Collection played.

The Mystics

1965

Collingullie Hall	Dec [?]	Freebie

1966

Wagga Police Boys Club	15th Jan [?]	Mystics/Shantines
Wagga Police Boys Club	29th Jan [?]	Mystics/Shantines
The Rock Hall	5th Feb [?]	First gig at The Rock – Des's last gig [?]
St John's Hall Wagga	12th Feb [?]	The girls didn't dance with the Sprogs!
The Rock Hall	7th April	Easter Thursday – a sad start to Easter
Lockhart Memorial Hall	9th April	Advertised as "The Rock Orchestra"
The Rock Hall	16th April	
The Rock Hall	30th Apr	
The Rock Hall	14th May	
The Rock Hall	29th May	

The following gigs were taken from Woody's 1966 Gig Book – June to December - no details of venues, simply that the band played on these dates. It would be reasonable to assume these gigs were most likely at The Rock [every two weeks], Lockhart, Yerong Creek and Collingullie.

The Rock Hall	4th June
	11th June
The Rock Hall	18th June
	25th Jun
The Rock Hall	9th July
	30th July
The Rock Hall	5th Aug
	6th Aug
	19th Aug
The Rock Hall	20th Aug
	26th Aug
	27th Aug
	2nd Sept
The Rock Hall	3rd Sept
	10th Sept
The Rock Hall	17th Sept
	24th Sept
The Rock Hall	8th Oct

The Rock Hall	27th Oct	Thursday – school dance [?]
The Rock Hall	12th Nov	
	18th Nov	
The Rock Hall	26th Nov	
	27th Nov	
	28th Nov	Monday [?]
Jerilderie Civic Hall	3rd Dec	
	20th Dec	Woody's new Vadis amp – "crap"!
The Rock Hall	24th Dec	Christmas Eve
Pleasant Hills Hall	31st Dec	Huge crowd – "Hot as shit"! Pub drank dry!

1967

	1st Jan	Woody's diary "Hangover - Pleasant Hills"!
The Rock Hall	28th Jan	Dance closed early due to cyclone warning
After 5 Club	11th Feb	Mick Walker's 21st – Woody's black eye!
Leagues Club Pac Lounge	18th Feb	Dianne Spence's 21st
Lockhart RSL Hall	24th Feb	Footy Club
The Rock Hall	25th Feb	Tasmania Bushfire Appeal – freebie
Yerong Creek Hall	4th Mar	Joyce Taylor's 21st
The Rock Hall	11th Mar	
Lockhart RSL Hall	18th Mar	
North Wagga Hall	25th Mar	John Herrington's 21st
Yerong Creek Hall	31st Mar	P&C Ball
The Rock Hall	1st Apr	
Lockhart Golf Club	8th April	
	15th April	Last appearance by The End
The Rock Hall	15th April	
Collingullie Hall	22nd April	BBQ and Dance
The Rock Hall	29th April	
Tootool	6th May	Vennell's Woolshed – The Rock Footy Club
After 5 Club	7th May	Mystics/Everchanging Minds
The Rock Hall	12th May	Kids Fancy Dress Ball
The Rock Hall	13th May	Seymour laryngitis, Porky injured
After 5 Club	14th May	Cancelled
Walla Walla Hall	19th May	Old boarding school town
The Rock Hall	27th May	
Lockhart Golf Club	3rd June	
After 5 Club	4th June	Seymour missing tooth – footy injury
Henty Memorial Hall	9th June	PFA Dance
Lake Albert Hall	10th June	21st
After 5 Club	11th June	
Henty Memorial Hall	17th June	Grand Opening – "The Fabulous Mystics"
The Rock Hall	18th June	
Grannies	24th June	Les missing tooth + stiches
	25th June	Battle of the Sounds[?]
Henty Memorial Hall	1st July	Mod dance
The Rock Hall	2nd July	

The Rock Hall	15th July	
Henty Memorial Hall	21st July	
Lockhart Golf Club	22nd July	
The Rock Hall	29th July	
The Rock Hall	12th Aug	
Henty Memorial Hall	19th Aug	Mod dance
The Rock Hall	26th Aug	
Boree Creek Hall	1st Sept	Thick fog on trip home
Lockhart RSL Hall	2nd Sept	
After 5 Club	3rd Sept	Daily Advertiser photo/Woody out
The Rock Hall	9th Sept	Pat in
Yerong Creek	16th Sept	Edward's Woolshed – great night
	15th Sept	Daily Advertiser photo/article in paper
The Rock Hall	23rd Sept	
After 5 Club	30th Sept	Midnight to dawn
The Rock Hall	7th Oct	
The Rock Hall	21st Oct	
Henty Memorial Hall	4th Nov	Mod dance
2WG Wollundry Room	5th Nov	Les's last gig!
Walla Walla Hall	10th Nov	Woody back!
The Rock Hall	11th Nov	
Henty Memorial Hall	17th Nov	
Jerilderie Civic Hall	18th Nov	Woody's diary - "fantastic"
After 5 Club	19th Nov	to see The Final Four
The Rock Hall	24th Nov	
St Joseph's Hall	25th Nov	YCW
The Rock Hall	1st Dec	
Kyeamba Smith Hall	2nd Dec	Mighty Mystics/Ronnie Burns
Lockhart Golf Club	9th Dec	advertised as "Mystics Orchestra"!
Culcairn Hall	15th Dec	
Lockhart Golf Club	20th Dec	
The Rock Hall	23rd Dec	Christmas Eve dance
The Rock Hall	30th Dec	
Kyeamba Smith Hall	31st Dec	Mystics/Climax 5/Bobby Thomas

1968

Wagga Mem Gardens	1st Jan	Mardi Gras/Seymour's voice stuffed
Kyeamba Smith Hall	6th Jan [?]	Mystics/Generation of Love
The Rock Hall	13th Jan	RSL Auxiliary
Subway Opening	20th Jan	Fabulous Mystics
Subway	21st Jan	Mystics/Izzy Di and Adrienne
Subway	28th Jan	Wagga's Own Mystics/Somebody's Image
Subway	17th Feb	Mystics 3-piece/Cherokees
Subway	24th Feb	Return of "The Mighty Mystics"
St Joseph's	1st Mar	YCW
Subway	2nd Mar	Mystics/Marty Rhone
Tumut C of E Hall	8th Mar	Tumut YAF

Book Book Hall Ball	9th Mar [?]	Book Book Tennis Club
Coolamon Golf Club	15th Mar [?]	B&S
Coolamon Private Prop	16th Mar [?]	B&S recovery – Newcastle gig offer
Subway	23rd Mar	
	28TH Mar	Subway becomes Noah's
Temora Town Hall	29th Mar	Mystics/Jon Blanchfield/Wimowehs
Noah's	30th Mar	Mystics/Jon Blanchfield/Laurie Allen
	1st April [?]	Seymour leaves, Jock in
	13th April	Noah's Fire - Easter
	15th April	The Shadows at the Plaza Theatre
The Rock Hall	11th May	Porky leaves, Dick in
Yerong Creek Hall	25th May	Rural Youth Club
St Joseph's	7th June	"the reappearance of The Mystics"
The Rock Hall	8th June	Woody arm in sling – finger injury
Henty Memorial Hall	14th June	
Pioneer Hall Tumbarumba	2nd Aug	The local lads after Jock!
The Klub	17th Aug	Mystics/The Exits – venue?
Pioneer Hall Tumbarumba	24th Aug	Jacky McGrath helps out/ Dick sick!
Pioneer Hall Tumbarumba	22nd Sept	
	7th Oct	Mystics reformed reported in paper
2WG Wollundry Room	5th Nov	Seymour/Porky in – Jock/Dick out

The Mystics reformed and renamed

Collection

Wesley Coffee Room	15th Nov	
	21st Nov	Paper - new name - Collection
Kyeamba Smith Hall	23rd Nov	Collection/Capt. Walker
The Rock Hall	29th Nov	
Wombat Wagga	6th Dec	
Batlow Literary Institute	7th Dec	Still advertised as The Mystics
Tumut Boys Club	14th Dec	"Wagga's popular band"
Wombat Wagga	21st Dec	RSL Hall
The Rock Hall	24th Dec	Younger Set
Wagga Country Club	31st Dec [?]	NYE dance – Seymour's Last gig [?]

1969

Kings Own Hotel	18th Jan	Unc in - Start 4 months residency
Pioneer Hall Tumbarumba	24th Jan	$85 – Woody hit sheep Ladysmith
Kings Own Hotel	25th Jan	$63
Lockhart Memorial Hall	31st Jan	
Kings Own Hotel	1st Feb	
Kings Own Hotel	8th Feb	
Lockhart Memorial Hall	14th Feb	"The Collections"
Kings Own Hotel	15th Feb	

A BAND FROM THE ROCK

Venue	Date	Notes
Lockhart Memorial Hall	21st Feb	"The Collections"
Kings Own Hotel	22nd Feb	
Holbrook B&S	28th Feb	Woody's diary - $180 two nights
Holbook B&S Recovery	1st Mar	
Lockhart Memorial Hall	7th Mar	
Kings Own Hotel	8th Mar	
Batlow Literary Institute	14th Mar	
Kings Own Hotel	15th Mar	
Book Book Hall	21st Mar	
Kings Own Hotel	22nd Mar	
Lockhart Memorial Hall	3rd April	"The Collections" - Thursday
Kings Own Hotel	5th April	
After 5 Club	6th April	Collection/Tin Soldiers
Broadway Theatre Junee	11th April	
Kings Own Hotel	12th April	
Kings Own Hotel	19th April	
Teacher's College	25th April	
Kings Own Hotel	26th April	
The Rock Hall	2nd May	Unc's first gig at the hall
Kyeamba Smith Hall	3rd May	Pacesetter
Batlow literary Institute	9th May	Advertised as "Collections"
Kings Own Hotel	10th May	
Batlow Literary Institute	16th May	
Holbrook	17th May	Porky stiches – "crowd go wild"
Wombat Tumut	24th May	
Broadway Theatre Junee	25th May	Sunday
St Joseph's	30th May	A very important date for Brownie!
Kyeamba Smith Hall	31st May	Pacesetter [Keith Bird]
St Joseph's	6th June	
Kyeamba Smith Hall	7th June	Pacesetter "Famous Collection"
Griffith RSL Hall	8th June	Keith Bird gig
Broadway Theatre Junee	13th June	Big Dance
Wagga RSL Downstairs	14th June	ANZ Staff Weekend
Gregadoo Hall	15th June	ANZ Staff Weekend
Kyeamba Smith Hall	20th June	Spinster's Ball – Paper photos
Griffith RSL Hall	21st June [?]	
	26th June	Photo/article in Daily Advertiser
Teacher's College	27th June	Ball
Holbrook	28th June	
Broadway Theatre Junee	4th July	
Kyeamba Smith Hall	5th July	
Wagga Civic Theatre	6th July	Battle of the Bands
St Joseph's	25th July	
Teacher's College	27th July	Afternoon concert
Broadway Theatre Junee	1st Aug	
Downside	2nd Aug	Monster Woolshed Dance and BBQ
Wagga High School	8th Aug	Ball
Kyeamba Smith Hall	15th Aug	Youth Rally – 1000 kids
Kyeamba Smith Hall	17th Aug	Sunday Pop Concert - 6 bands
Broadway Theatre	22nd Aug	

Ganmain Hall	23rd Aug		Great crowd
Broadway Theatre	29th Aug		Ball – with the girlfriends
Downside Hall	30th Aug		Dance/BBQ – "Fabulous Collection"
Griffith RSL Hall	4th Sept		Crowd of around 400
Pioneer Hall Tumbarumba	6th Sep		Festival of the Mountain Gums
St Joseph's	12th Sep		
Myall Park Hall	13th Sep	[?]	B&S
Wesley Cabaret Room	19th Sep		
Kyeamba Smith Hall	20th Sep		YCW – Sunday night
Wesley Church	28th Sep		Youth church service
Griffith RSL Hall	10th Oct		
Ganmain Hall	17th Oct		
Kyeamba Smith Hall	19th Oct		YCW – Sunday night
	6th Nov		Daily Advertiser - hint re changes
Wombat Wagga	8th Nov		"Wagga's top group"
Wesley Cabaret Room	9th Nov		
	15th Nov		Wedding – Unc/Denitsa [2 weeks off]
Pioneer Hall Tumbarumba	29th Nov		
The Rock Hall	30th Nov		
Wagga Aerodrome	5th Dec	[?]	Young National Party gig
Wombat Wagga	7th Dec		Sunday
Wesley Cabaret Room	12th Dec		
Wombat Tumut	14th Dec		Sunday night
Junee RSL Hall	20th Dec		YCW
The Rock Hall	24th Dec		Last gig for Porky and Brownie

Gig Summary

Single gig weekends	x 87	=	87
2 gig weekends	x 54	=	108
3 gig weekends	x 8	=	24
Total Gigs		=	219

Gig Venues

Gigs – Wagga

Kyeamba Smith Hall	=	13
Subway/Noah's	=	8
After 5 Club	=	7
St Joseph's	=	7
Wombat Wagga	=	4
Wesley Cabaret Room	=	4
Teacher's College	=	3
2WG Wollundry Room	=	2
Police Boy's Club	=	2
Wagga Country Club	=	1

Wagga Aerodrome	=	1
Civic Theatre	=	1
Memorial Gardens	=	1
The Klub	=	1
Leagues Club P'fic Lounge	=	1
North Wagga Hall	=	1
Lake Albert Hall	=	1
Grannies	=	1
St John's Hall	=	1
Gregadoo Hall	=	1
Wagga High School	=	1
Wesley Church	=	1
Wagga RSL [d'stairs]	=	1 [both bands played private functions here]

Gigs - The Rock
- Masonic Hall = 50
- Kings Own Hotel = 14

Gigs – Lockhart
- RSL/Memorial Hall = 9
- Golf Club = 5

Gigs – Henty
- Memorial Hall = 8

Gigs – Junee
- Broadway Theatre = 7
- RSL Hall = 1

Gigs – Other
- Pioneer Hall Tumbarumba = 6
- Holbrook/ Mullengandra = 4
- Yerong Creek = 4
- Batlow Institute = 4
- Griffith RSL Hall = 4
- Tumut Wombat = 2
- Walla Walla = 2
- Jerilderie Civic Hall = 2
- Book Book Hall = 2
- Coolamon = 2
- Ganmain = 2
- Downside = 2
- Collingullie = 2
- Pleasant Hills Hall = 1
- Tootool = 1
- Culcairn = 1
- Boree Creek = 1
- Myall Park, Griffith = 1
- Temora = 1
- Tumut Boys Club = 1
- Tumut C of E Hall = 1
- Uranquinty = 1

Gigs - Venue not identified = 14

Total Gigs = 219

<u>There are two blots on the gig guide</u> –

The Swimming Pool Committee did not advertise dances at The Rock Hall in any local paper and totally relied on Julie McGrath's posters, and word of mouth. Dances at Lockhart could not be traced for 1967 and 1968 due to there being no copies of the Lockhart paper, a period when the band played regularly in the supper room of the Lockhart Memorial Hall and at the Lockhart Golf Club.

Woody's diaries partly solved the problems above by providing the following –
1966 - gig dates only June – Dec 1966
1967 - detailed gig dates excluding Sept – Nov 1967
1968 – diary not found
1969 - detailed gig dates Jan - July 1969

There are still gaps and as can be seen from the above, there are about 23 months in total during the 4 years the bands were going where gig dates were not available from Woody's diaries. The period after the Noah's fire is very sparse for identified gigs despite Jock's recollection that The Mystics worked regularly when he and Dick were in the band. Whilst Collection played more gigs in 1969 than in any preceding year, the gap in Woody's diary for the latter part of that year means that there would have been gigs that could not be otherwise identified. Consequently, it is possible in the 23 months there could be upwards of 30-40 gigs over the 4 years that could have been added to the Gig Guide.

A BAND FROM THE ROCK

The Mystics 1966 – 1968

Seymour

Woody

Les

Porky

Brownie

Pat

The Mystics Gig Ads

Collection 1969

Unc

Pat

Woody

Porky

Brownie

Collection Gig Ads

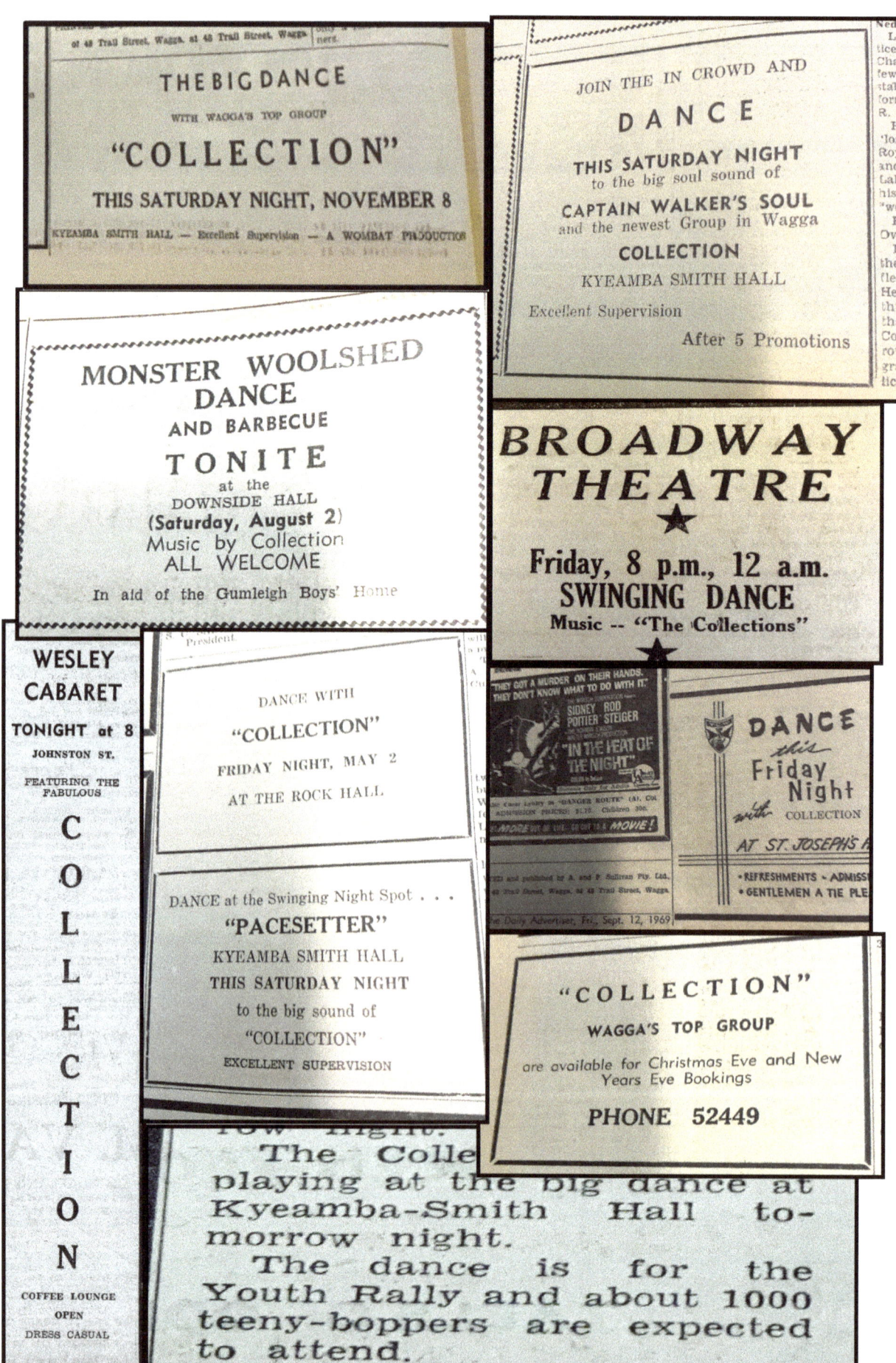

A BAND FROM THE ROCK

Various Gig Ads – The Mystics and Collection

DANCING
8.30 p.m. to 12.30.
"The Collections" band
Lockhart Memorial Hall
Friday 21st February

GRAND OPENING —
HENTY MOD DANCE
TOMORROW NIGHT
Saturday, 17th June.
Memorial Hall, Henty.
Dancing 8 to 12 Midnight.
Music by Fabulous Mystics.

50-50 DANCE
in aid of Tumbarumba Festival Funds
PIONEER HALL, TUMBARUMBA
Saturday, September 6
Music by "The Collection"
REFRESHMENTS

DANCE
AT WESLEY HALL and COFFEE ROOM
Corner Johnston and Tarcutta Streets
TONIGHT AT 8 O'CLOCK
MUSIC BY COLLECTION

DANCE
EASTER SATURDAY NIGHT, APRIL 9
Memorial Hall Supper Room
The Rock Orchestra
Cool drinks available

LOCKHART GOLF CLUB
SPECIAL CHRISTMAS SOCIAL PARTY
AT CLUB HOUSE
SATURDAY, 9th DECEMBER, 1967
8.30 pm
MEMBERS AND INVITED GUESTS CORDIALLY WELCOMED
MYSTICS ORCHESTRA   SUPPER

Entertainment
TEENAGE DANCE
PIONEER HALL TUMBARUMBA
Next Friday night January 24
MUSIC BY "THE COLLECTION"

BROADWAY THEATRE
LONG WEEKEND ATTRACTIONS
Friday
BIG DANCE
Music by the Collections

LOCKHART MEMORIAL HALL
Thursday, April 3
Dancing 8 p.m. till Midnight
THE COLLECTIONS

HENTY MOD DANCE
TOMORROW NIGHT
Saturday, 19th August.
Henty Memorial Hall.
Dancing 8 p.m. - 12 Midnight to the sound of the "MYSTICS."

OUR SUNDAY NIGHT SPOT
E AFTER 5 CLUB
Music by "THE MYSTICS"

DANCE
TO THE MYSTICS ON 14th JUNE
HENTY MEMORIAL HALL.
Admission, 80 Cents   Supper Provided.
Sponsored by the Henty Rotary Club in aid of the Henty Central School Library.

The Mystics

A BAND FROM THE ROCK

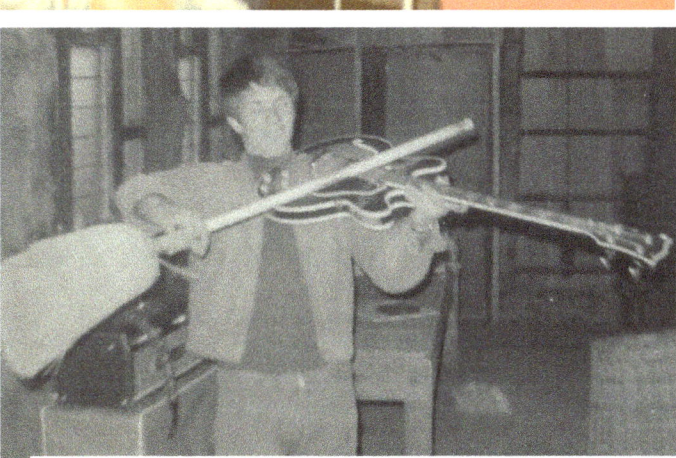

POP MUSIC

A pop group and a football team may seem to have no connection.

But four members of The Rock-Yerong Creek Australian Rules football team play for the Mystics, one of the district's leading pop groups.

The group which was formed two years ago, has attracted a wide following since it first began playing at teenage dances.

All five members of the group come from The Rock area, but during the week work at different occupations.

Peter Brown, 19, bass guitar, works in an insurance office in Wagga.

Dennis McGrath, 19, drums, and Les Magrath, 19, rythm guitar, are both P.M.G. technicians during the week — Dennis at Jerilderie and Les in Wagga.

Vocalist for the group, 17-year-old Col Moore, works on his father's farm near The Rock.

Lead guitarist Rod Finlayson, 18, is in his sixth year at Wagga High School, but lives at Yerong Creek.

When interviewed at a Sunday dance recently, Peter said they aimed at a commercial sound in their music.

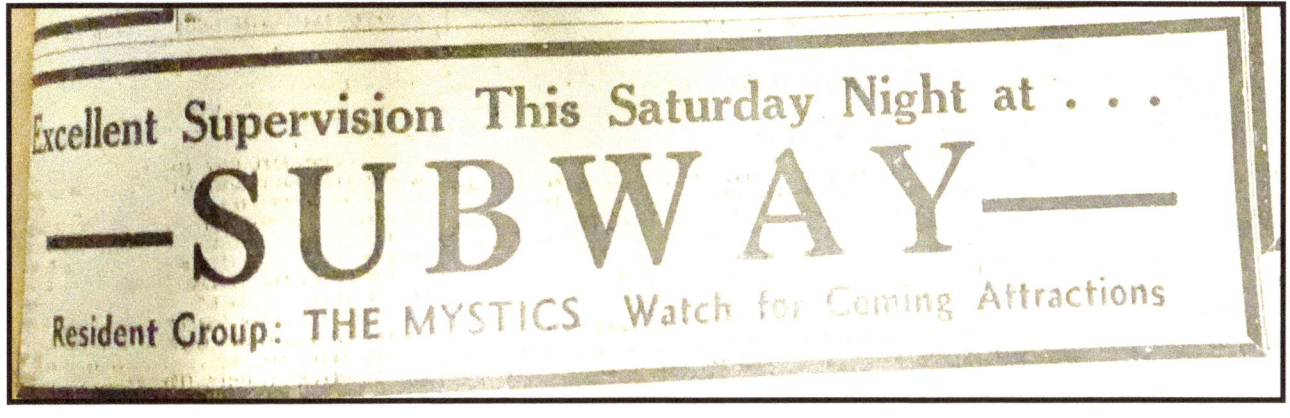

Collection

THE BIG DANCE

WITH WAGGA'S TOP GROUP

"COLLECTION"

THIS SATURDAY NIGHT, NOVEMBER 8

KYEAMBA SMITH HALL — Excellent Supervision — A WOMBAT PRODUCTION

Odds and Sods

WESLEY CABARET
TONIGHT at 8
JOHNSTON ST.
FEATURING THE FABULOUS
COLLECTION
COFFEE LOUNGE
OPEN
DRESS CASUAL

The Collection is moving into the ball scene in a big way, catering for the slightly older age group.

This follows a successful 3½ months at the Kings Own Hotel at The Rock, where the group has attracted a regular following.

Last Friday night the boys played at the Teachers' College in Wagga, where it was a really swinging night.

The newest member of the group, singer Colin Moses, is said to be fitting in well with the other members' sound.

This weekend The Collection will be playing at The Rock and Kyeamba Smith Hall.

Dennis McGrath....(Ex Drummer for COLLECTION)
31st December, '69....

No idea who the singer is or where this gig was!

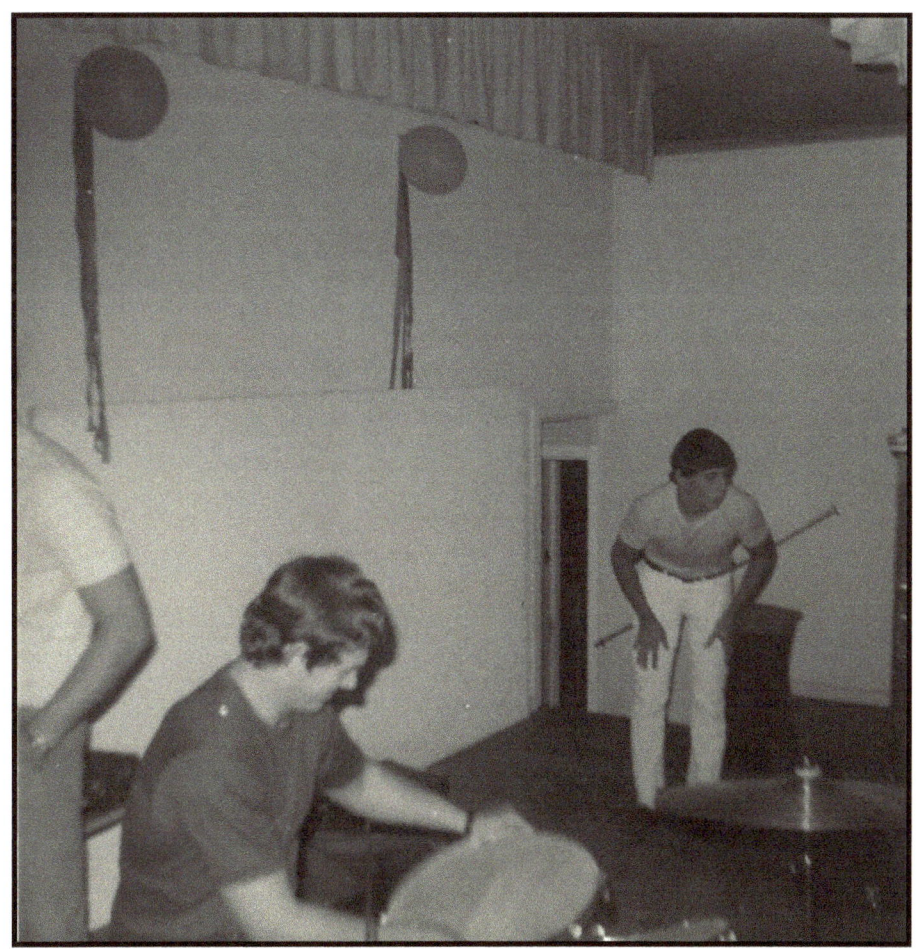

Porky remembers balloons up on the walls of the Civic Hall at our 1st gig
in Jerilderie so it is likely the other person in the photo
must be the DJ who compered the night.

YOUR SUNDAY NIGHT SPOT

THE AFTER 5 CLUB

Music by "THE MYSTICS"

Wombat's next do at the Kyeamba Smith Hall will feature Wagga group The Collection, on Saturday night.

The 2007 [and final] Reunion Concert

The 2007 Reunion Concert "ring-ins"!

Dave Wall

Nick Freeman

what a night

Following The Rock and District Aged Care Committee 60s night fund raiser held at Kyeamba Smith Hall in Wagga on Saturday, I wish to express my heartfelt thanks firstly to the 850 patrons who joined with us in this fantastic trip down memory lane.

Some people travelled from as far afield as Western Australia, Canberra, Melbourne, Sydney and beyond and I'm sure they are going home with memories that will last a lifetime.

The night was an absolute sensation and far outweighed our highest expectations.

The Mystics/Collection band were every bit as good and probably better than they were in 1965 and they certainly did us proud – they were sensational and mere words can't really express our gratitude to this group of wonderful musicians.

Letter to the Editor,
Wagga Daily Advertiser
2005 Reunion Concert

Now for my bit!

The following are included for their historical, rather than their musical, significance and because I put this whole story together!

"Collection" had a bit of a setback on the weekend when "Woody" Finlayson, their rhythm guitarist lost his voice.

So, sweet harmonies were supplied by bass guitarist Peter Brown.

On Friday, the group played at Griffith to a crowd of nearly 400.

Tomorrow night they will be playing at the dance at St. Joseph's Hall.

There is one hopefully compensatory factor in all the above – that my bass playing made up for any other musical short-coming!!

Finally - I suppose it's the thought that counts!

> Hi Pete
>
> I've put this in big letters so you can read it.
>
> Georgie asked me if I had some memorabilia to send for your birthday. Remembered I had an old two track tape of us in your bedroom at The Rock with you on double bass and me playing a toothbrush holder recorded maybe 68 or 69.
>
> I found the tape. I have the original two track recording machine.
>
> It won't play. It's dead. Tried the tape in my old 4 track machine.
>
> It won't play. It's dead. The tape broke.
>
> So as a special gift I send you what could be the original tape of that momentous session. It may be on this tape or may be not.
>
> I don't know what's on it but it's yours to keep.
>
> Bear in mind it is a great sacrifice for me to give away royalties for this recording but due to the momentous occasion of you turning 70 I am happy to oblige.
>
> Try running it through your computer, toaster or microwave to see wh on it.
>
> If it won't work the thought was there.
>
> Happy Birthday my friend.
>
> > We should have a meeting next year after April for those of us who made it to 70.
>
> > Cheers
> > Wood.

Woody's letter to me on my 70th Birthday in 2018

The long-lost tape of Woody and me in my bedroom circa 1966/67 – I didn't trust Woody's suggestions re computer, toaster and microwave so put it through a washing machine cycle which should clean up the sound quality!

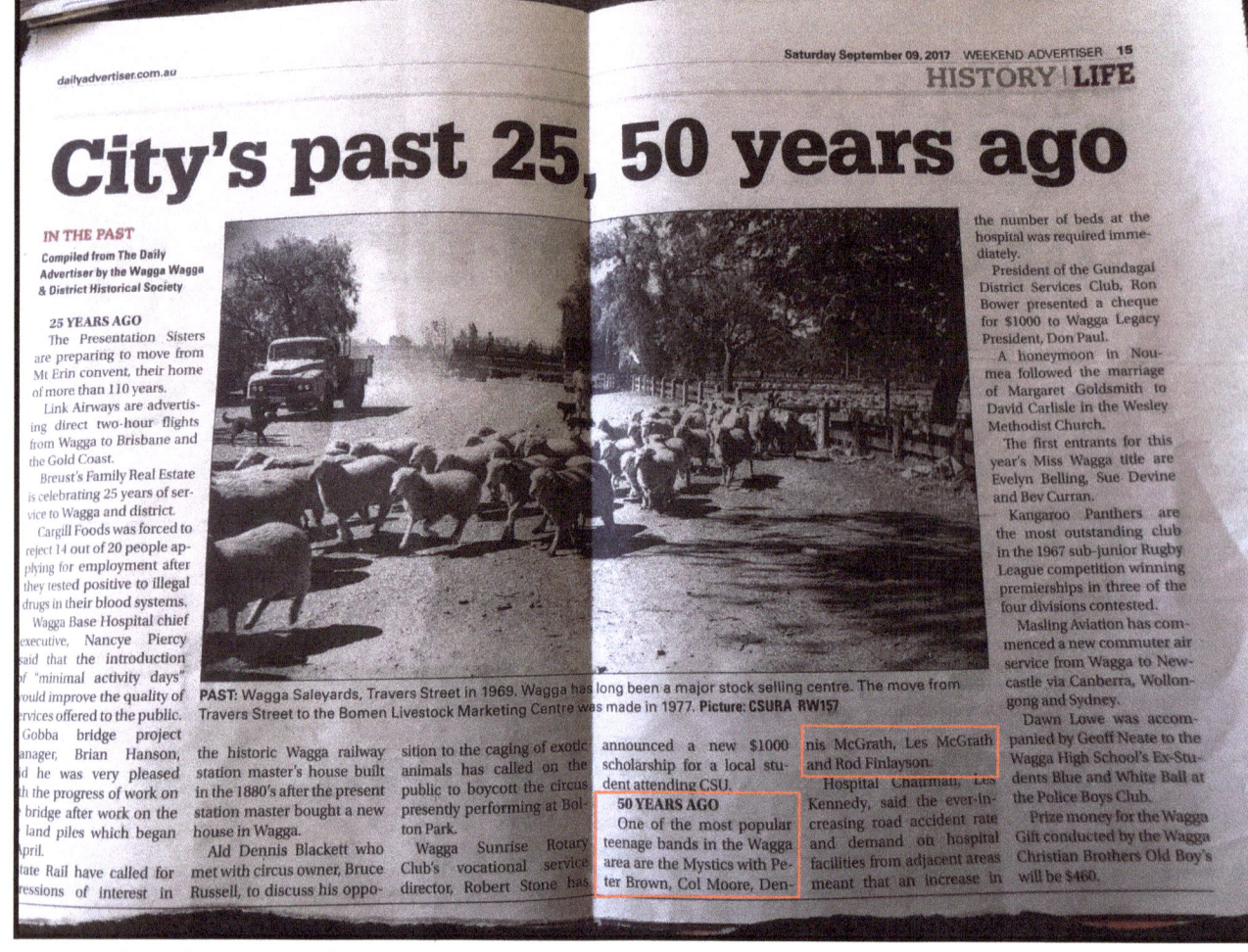

The above article appeared in the Wagga Daily Advertiser's weekly *City's Past, 25 and 50 Years Ago* section in September 2017, 50 years to the week that The Mystics appeared at The After 5 Club in 1967.

Below is Eminar Amplifiers advertisement from "Go Set" Magazine 26th December 1968 – some very good musos mentioned!

The author – 2007 Reunion Concert
Wagga Daily Advertiser photo

After completing his high school education, Peter Brown joined the General Insurance profession, initially working for a large well-known Australian Insurance company. After a couple of years, he applied successfully for transfer to the company's operation in Papua New Guinea and spent two years from the middle of 1970 working at the company's offices in Rabaul, Port Moresby and Lae. He returned to Wagga Wagga in late 1972 and after 15 years, resigned and set up his own Insurance Broking company which continues today under family management, and which is part of a large ASX listed entity.

His interest in music started whilst he was still at school in 1965 when he got his first electric bass guitar and his involvement in music continues to the present. He has played in pop, rock, country and jazz groups, old-time and big bands, has recorded on albums, played in stage and theatre pit bands as well as in special event backing bands.

He took up the double bass in the early 1990s and over the next 20 years played with pick-up and feature groups at regional jazz festivals in NSW and Victoria.

He was most recently an integral member of a group of local musicians who performed tribute concerts under the Classic Bands/Classic Albums banner over a number of years

He is married to June and has four children. He retired in 2019 and spends most of his time waiting for the next gig offer.

www.ingramcontent.com/pod-product-compliance
Lightning Source LLC
Chambersburg PA
CBHW061056170426
43194CB00025B/2959